Education and Child Welfare System Efforts to Improve Educational Outcomes for Youth in Foster Care

Identifying Opportunities to Enhance Cross-System Collaboration

SUSAN BUSH-MECENAS, HEATHER GOMEZ-BENDAÑA, DIONNE BARNES-PROBY, SUSAN M. GATES

RAND EDUCATION AND LABOR

For more information on this publication, visit **www.rand.org/t/RRA2373-1**.

About RAND

The RAND Corporation is a research organization that develops solutions to public policy challenges to help make communities throughout the world safer and more secure, healthier and more prosperous. RAND is nonprofit, nonpartisan, and committed to the public interest. To learn more about RAND, visit www.rand.org.

Research Integrity

Our mission to help improve policy and decisionmaking through research and analysis is enabled through our core values of quality and objectivity and our unwavering commitment to the highest level of integrity and ethical behavior. To help ensure our research and analysis are rigorous, objective, and nonpartisan, we subject our research publications to a robust and exacting quality-assurance process; avoid both the appearance and reality of financial and other conflicts of interest through staff training, project screening, and a policy of mandatory disclosure; and pursue transparency in our research engagements through our commitment to the open publication of our research findings and recommendations, disclosure of the source of funding of published research, and policies to ensure intellectual independence. For more information, visit www.rand.org/about/research-integrity.

RAND's publications do not necessarily reflect the opinions of its research clients and sponsors.

Published by the RAND Corporation, Santa Monica, Calif.
© 2023 RAND Corporation
RAND® is a registered trademark.

Library of Congress Cataloging-in-Publication Data is available for this publication.
ISBN: 978-1-9774-1091-7

Cover image: fstop123/Getty Images

Limited Print and Electronic Distribution Rights

About This Report

In this report, we examine the context for cross-system collaboration between the education and child welfare systems to improve the educational outcomes of youth in foster care. This report was internally funded through the RAND Corporation and is intended as a first step toward understanding how governance features influence cross-system collaboration and identifying directions for future research. Our findings and recommendations to federal, state, and local policymakers are based on exploratory research conducted through a combination of methods, including policy review, data scan, and qualitative case study.

RAND Education and Labor

This research was undertaken by RAND Education and Labor, a division of the RAND Corporation that conducts research on early childhood through postsecondary education programs, workforce development, and programs and policies affecting workers, entrepreneurship, and financial literacy and decisionmaking.

More information about RAND can be found at www.rand.org. Questions about this should be directed to Susan_Gates@rand.org, and questions about RAND Education and Labor should be directed to educationandlabor@rand.org.

Funding

Funding for this research was provided by gifts from RAND supporters and income from operations.

Acknowledgments

We are extremely grateful to the education and child welfare agency representatives and adults who have experience in foster care who offered their perspectives and insights in our interviews and focus groups. Their time and willingness to share their experiences are invaluable for this effort and for helping us understand how to better support their work. We are also grateful to the members of our advisory panel, who provided invaluable feedback on directions and design of our research and reacted to emerging findings. Members of the advisory panel were Jane Clark, Data Quality Campaign; Janay Eustace, California Youth Connection; Michelle Francois, National Center for Youth Law; Aakanksha Sinha, Casey Family Programs; Scott Richardson and Bryan Thurmond, liaisons, U.S. Department of Education; and Traci Williams, Los Angeles Unified School District. Although advisory panel members provided valuable input and feedback, their involvement should not be interpreted as approval of the report by them or their employers. We thank our peer reviewers, Peter Pecora of the Casey Family Programs and the University of Washington School of Social Work and Christopher Nelson of RAND, for their helpful feedback that greatly improved this report. We also thank Melissa Parmelee for her editorial expertise and Monette Velasco for overseeing the publication process for this report.

Summary

Youth in foster care face numerous challenges that make it more difficult for them to achieve aspects of adult life that many take for granted: a stable home, a steady job, and good health. Educational attainment might increase the odds of success, but the educational outcomes of youth in foster care are far worse than those of other students. Transitions into or out of the foster care system, as well as placement changes, can lead to school transfers. Frequent school changes have been associated with a host of problems that contribute to this opportunity gap.

Since the early 2000s, policymakers at the state and federal levels have passed legislation designed to promote collaboration between the education and child welfare systems, with the goal of improving the educational stability of youth in foster care and, in turn, their educational outcomes. Even though the value of cross-system collaboration is intuitive and broadly acknowledged, implementing cross-system collaboration locally—never mind scaling it—has posed challenges. Why is this implementation so difficult?

Two features of public-sector systems in the United States might pose barriers to cross-system collaboration: (1) fragmentation within systems and (2) jurisdictional misalignment across systems. In this report, we explore the implications of fragmentation and misalignment for cross-system collaboration between kindergarten through grade 12 (K–12) public education and child welfare systems. We looked at the extent to which fragmentation of responsibilities within each system and alignment of those responsibilities across systems within a state present barriers to and opportunities for cross-system collaboration.

Approach

Our research relied on a combination of methods, including policy review, data scan, and qualitative case study. The policy review focused on three key federal policies governing collaboration between these two systems: the Every Student Succeeds Act, the Fostering Connections to Success and Increasing Adoptions Act, and the McKinney-Vento Homeless Assistance Act. The data scan involved collecting publicly available data on the governance features of the education and child welfare systems across the United States. We conducted case studies in four states, which were selected to demonstrate variation in these governance features. These case studies included interviews with education and child welfare system representatives across multiple levels, focus groups with adults who were previously in foster care, and policy and document review. We analyzed data from these sources to examine the factors that enable or constrain collaboration across the systems.

Key Findings

We found that, while federal legislation shapes efforts at the state and local levels to support youth in foster care and other student populations served by both systems, states differ in how they structure the governance of their education and child welfare systems. This variation influences the need and opportunities for collaboration. Adults who have experienced foster care noted the importance of student and caregiver involvement in processes set up to identify the best educational placement for a student, a caring person who served as a point of contact at school, and assistance in identifying and accessing education-related resources. Case data suggest several factors that contributed to or inhibited collaboration between systems:

- Most interagency and interpersonal communication focuses on developing consistent understanding of existing policy and managing special cases.
- Formalization through legislation and routines forges shared understanding and allows for meaningful information-sharing.
- Some jurisdictions we studied use unique methods to promote collaboration, including creation of meaningful liaison roles, opportunities for district liaisons and caseworkers to develop social connections, integration of best interest determination guidance on school notification forms, and accountability-linked data-sharing.
- Common challenges include high staff turnover, limited preservice training on educational stability for youth in foster care, and geographical dispersion.

Recommendations

Although our report is exploratory, it points to some policy considerations at the local, state, and federal levels, as well as directions for future research.

At the **local level**, policymakers can encourage collaboration, information-sharing, and transparency to support those working most directly with youth in foster care by

- removing barriers that restrict access to the information needed to support youth in foster care
- incentivizing and facilitating cross-system communication and social engagement
- designating a contact or hotline for youth or caregivers who need assistance with school stability concerns.

At the **state level**, policymakers can promote standard operating procedures and create resources and templates that would facilitate effective collaboration between local actors and relieve them of the burden of creating such procedures from scratch by

- requiring written dispute resolution for service provisions related to youth in foster care
- providing joint guidance defining and serving youth in foster care
- providing statewide standard tools, procedures, and definitions—especially with regard to data-sharing and placement decisions
- including educational outcomes for youth in foster care as school accountability indicators
- using youth-centered data metrics
- integrating education stability training into basic caseworker preparation.

At the **federal level**, policymakers can further encourage collaboration by

- allocating a designated funding mechanism for students in foster care
- using and encouraging best practices that have worked at a state level.

Our exploratory analysis suggests several areas in which additional research would help support better collaboration between child welfare and education systems focused on the educational outcomes of youth in foster care. A systematic policy review of the varied definitions of youth in foster care and their transitions might help to show where a lack of policy coherence poses challenges for collaboration. Inquiry into the benefits and drawbacks of consistent school placement could illuminate the factors that influence best placement for youth and the practice of caseworkers who support the educational opportunities and outcomes of youth. Finally, because policy emphasizes the role of states in supporting cross-system collaboration, it might be worth examining how both cross-system and within-system collaboration work when transitions cross state lines.

Contents

Figure and Tables

Figure

Tables

CHAPTER 1

Introduction

Youth in foster care face numerous challenges that make it more difficult for them to achieve aspects of adult life that many take for granted—a stable home, a steady job, and good health (Pecora et al., 2005; Barrat and Berliner, 2013). Although educational attainment is associated with improved outcomes, youth in foster care have substantially lower rates of high school completion and bachelor's degree attainment than other students (Pecora and O'Brien, 2019).

Evidence suggests that a majority of school-age children in foster care have experienced multiple foster care placements (Pecora and O'Brien, 2019). Moves associated with transitions into or out of the foster care system, as well as placement changes, can lead to school changes. Frequent school changes, referred to as *high school mobility*, have been associated with a host of problems that contribute to an opportunity gap, which is reflected in increased risk of dropping out, repeating a grade, and having lower measures of achievement (standardized test scores, high school graduation rates, college enrollment, college persistence rates, etc.) (Zetlin, Weinberg, and Shea, 2010; Pecora, 2012; Clemens, Lalonde, and Sheesley, 2016; Pecora and O'Brien, 2019). Studies estimate that, on average, a young person in foster care might take up to six months to recover academically from each placement change (McKellar and Cowen, 2011). The lack of educational stability also disrupts the ability of youth in foster care to connect with their peers and teachers and have regular access to academic supports (Barrat and Berliner, 2013). Of note, Black and Latinx youth in foster care typically experience more school changes than their White peers in foster care (Pecora and O'Brien, 2019).

There is growing recognition about the challenges facing students in foster care and strategies to address these challenges. But the educational outcomes of youth in foster care, although valued by both the child welfare system and the education system, are not the primary focus of either system. Youth in foster care make up a very small minority in an education system that prioritizes parental involvement and privacy (Henderson and Mapp, 2002; Zinth, 2005; Hlavac and Easterly, 2015; Chen, 2022). As of September 2021, just over 391,000 youth in the United States were in foster care, compared with public school enrollment of nearly 50 million youth (Children's Bureau, 2022). For the child welfare system, educational outcomes for youth in foster care constitute only a small part of much broader goals of child safety and child and family well-being (Stoltzfus, 2019; National Center for Education Statistics, 2022a).

Since the early 2000s, policymakers at the state and federal levels have passed legislation designed to promote collaboration between the education and child welfare systems, with the goal of improving the education stability of youth in foster care and, in turn, their educational outcomes (National Conference of State Legislatures, 2016). A survey of foster care system stakeholders in Kansas highlighted shortfalls in cross-system collaboration as a key barrier to improving educational outcomes of students in foster care given the interrelated nature of these two systems (e.g., home placement changes have implications for school attendance, transportation, and student support) (Garstka et al., 2014). Despite progress because of legislative change, calls for improved collaboration endure (Schomburg and Ryder, 2022).

Research and academic publications on cross-sector collaboration between the education and child welfare systems focus on describing the need for and potential benefits of better cross-sector collaboration and describing examples of successful or promising collaborative practices, often on specific topics (for example, Burns et al., 2022). A few studies have explored barriers to collaboration or probed how and why those barriers may vary by context. For example, Langworthy and Robertson found that education and child welfare practitioners in three states "regularly faced challenges in navigating multiple school districts and county organizations, which each have unique rules and systems for data gathering, sharing and use" (Langworthy and Robertson, 2014, p. 5). That work suggested that the number of school districts in a state, urbanicity, and cultural differences between professionals in the respective systems influenced the ease of collaboration. A survey of system professionals in Minnesota conducted in 2013 suggested that time and lack of understanding other system and confidentiality requirements were key barriers to collaboration, that barriers and challenges vary based on the local context within the state, and that communication and relationship-building are key to successful collaboration (Langworthy and Larson, 2014).

This issue is just one of many complicated policy challenges for which there is broad recognition that cross-system collaboration is needed to move the needle. We define *cross-system collaboration* as organizations or individuals from different systems working together toward a shared goal. In this case, the shared goal is improving educational outcomes for youth in foster care. Even though the idea of cross-system collaboration is both prevalent and intuitive, implementing cross-system collaboration locally—never mind scaling it—has posed challenges. Why is this implementation so difficult?

Two features of public-sector systems in the United States pose barriers to cross-system collaboration: (1) fragmentation *within* systems and (2) jurisdictional misalignment *across* systems. Fragmentation within systems can create ambiguity about who is being asked to engage in cross-system collaboration and impede the implementation of desired actions. Jurisdictional misalignment across systems can limit the feasibility of collaboration, depending on whether the entities being asked to collaborate have the decisionmaking authority, expertise, resources, and incentives to collaborate.

Fragmentation is reflected in the number of local-government entities providing particular services or engaged in an activity. Fragmented functions typically involve many local-government entities, while consolidated functions involve few. In the United States, many of the most-critical public-sector systems, including law enforcement, education, child welfare, and mental health, are considered highly fragmented (see Goodman, 2019, for additional details). For example, in 2016 there were just over 12,000 local police agencies in the United States, and almost half of these agencies employed fewer than ten officers (Hyland and Davis, 2019). Active policy debates continue about whether to eliminate, overlap, or consolidate service provision in the name of efficiency, effectiveness, or equity.[1] The implications of fragmentation and jurisdictional misalignment for cross-system collaboration have not been a focus of academic research. *Misalignment* refers to differences between systems in the way resources, responsibilities, and authorities are assigned to hierarchical levels. For example, if two systems assign resources, responsibilities, and authorities to a county-level agency, the two systems would reflect strong alignment. However, if one system assigns resources, responsibilities, and authorities to school districts and the other system assigns them to the state or county, the two systems would not reflect strong alignment. We hypothesize that both fragmentation and jurisdictional misalignment are contextual elements that could influence the feasibility and success of collaborations (see, for example, Capacity Building Center for States, 2017).

Goal of This Report

With this report, we aim to shed light on models of collaboration and to understand the potential implications of fragmentation and misalignment for cross-system collaboration. Although the focus of our study was on collaboration between kindergarten through grade 12 (K–12) public education and child welfare systems to support the educational needs of youth in foster care or at risk of entering foster care, we hope that our findings may offer insights relevant to other cross-sector collaborations, such as those between law enforcement and mental health systems; shed light on other public-sector collaborative efforts; and contribute to the understanding of how the respective agencies collaborate. We explore the following research questions:

1. How do the degree of fragmentation of responsibilities within each system and the alignment of those responsibilities across systems

---

[1] Research on this topic tends to focus on *within-system* efficiency, equity, and distributional implications. When looking across systems and context, findings are mixed, which suggests both pros and cons to fragmentation (Martin and Schiff, 2011; Goodman, 2019). That said, targeted analyses have revealed some downsides to fragmentation, including racial segregation and cost (Krimmel, 1997; Ayscue and Orfield, 2015).

within a state present barriers and opportunities for cross-system collaboration?

2. What other factors contribute to barriers and opportunities for cross-system collaboration?

3. What strategies support cross-system collaboration, and how do these strategies vary depending on context?

Method Overview and Limitations

We address these questions through a combination of methods, including a policy review, data scan, qualitative case study, and engagement with an external advisory panel. These are described in greater detail in the appendix. The panel was composed of seven individuals from six organizations at the federal, state, and local levels who play different roles supporting the educational outcomes of youth in foster care, and each brings a different perspective to the topic. These organizations consisted of government, advocacy, and philanthropic organizations. Feedback from the external advisory panel informed the theoretical framework, guiding questions, and case selection methods. The panel also reviewed and provided comments on this publication.

In the policy review, we focused on three key federal policies governing collaboration between the education and child welfare systems: the Every Student Succeeds Act (ESSA) (Pub. L. 114-95, 2015), the Fostering Connections to Success and Increasing Adoptions Act (Pub. L. 110-351, 2008), and the McKinney-Vento Homeless Assistance Act (Pub. L. 100-77, 1987). In the data scan, we collected publicly available data on the governance features of the education and child welfare systems across the United States. Our team compiled information on governance, funding, enrollment, safety and permanence, and key policies for both the education and child welfare systems in all U.S. states and territories. These data were analyzed to examine the prevalence and variation of governance arrangements across the country. These data also informed case study selection.

Finally, we conducted case studies in four states, which were selected to demonstrate variation in these governance features. The case studies involved policy and document review, interviews with education and child welfare system representatives across multiple levels, and focus groups with adults who were previously in foster care. We reached out for interviews with a state, county or regional, and district or local representative from both education and child welfare agencies in each state. In total, we reached out to 39 individuals to request participation in interviews. Thirteen individuals agreed to participate in interviews.

In addition, in all four states, we reached out to advocacy organizations for youth in foster care and university support programs for adults who have been in foster care. Through these organizations, we invited adults (people older than 18 years of age) who had previously experienced foster care to join focus groups about their experience with the education and child welfare systems. In total, we conducted group interviews with 12 individuals. We conducted these semistructured interviews and focus groups from May 2022 through September 2022, via a video conference platform.

We analyzed data from these sources to examine the factors that enable or constrain collaboration across the two systems. All interviews were audio-recorded and transcribed. Transcribed data were then coded using a combination of deductively and inductively determined codes. We used cross-case meta-matrices to engage in systematic data reduction and to look for patterns across our case study sites. We then conducted analytic memoing, focusing on both within-case and across-case themes. Where possible, we triangulated interview findings with documentation. The study protocols were reviewed and approved by RAND's Human Subjects Protection Committee.

We consider this study exploratory in nature. There are limitations to the generalizability and validity of our data. First, we sampled just four states as case studies because of capacity constraints. Given the variation in policy and contexts across the country, our findings might not represent the experience of all states, counties, or local agencies. Second, we were unable to recruit participants across all levels of each case study system and did not sample representatives from nonprofits or community-based organizations that may commonly work with both systems. We believe that competing demands on time, particularly in the coronavirus disease 2019 (COVID-19) pandemic period, may have prohibited potential participants from joining the study. Therefore, we cannot systematically draw conclusions about cross- and within-system collaboration in all of the case states. Finally, our qualitative data collection draws on perception data, which may or may not fully reflect actual practice.

Organization of This Report

In the next chapter, we describe our conceptualization of the features of each system that have potential to influence *cross-system collaboration*, which we define as two or more agencies working together toward shared goals. Following this model, in Chapter 3 we describe the existing federal policy governing the education of youth in foster care. In Chapter 4, we examine how governance features vary across all states, using publicly available data. Drawing on that analysis, we explore ways in which education and child welfare agencies work together in four states that reflect different governance models and describe strategies these agencies have used to promote collaboration. We close with policy considerations and directions for future research in Chapter 5.

CHAPTER 2

Conceptualizing the Influence of Governance on Collaboration

To understand collaboration between the education and child welfare systems, we first consulted the extant literature. We began with the understanding that collaboration occurs both *across* systems (cross-system collaboration) and *within* systems across different levels (within-system collaboration). For each system, there are four levels at which functions might be executed and decisions made: local, county, regional, and state. The two dimensions of collaboration (cross-system and within-system) are intertwined in the sense that collaboration may span and vary across all levels of each system. Figure 2.1 draws on prior research to illustrate governance arrangements and other factors that influence within-system collaboration between education systems and child welfare systems.

As shown in Figure 2.1, we conceptualize cross-system collaboration as working toward the goal of supporting the educational attainment and success of youth in foster care. Note that the local systems may involve public and private schools and child welfare agencies. This process combines the separate strands of the education and child welfare systems (shown as split paths that might meet if cross-system collaboration is implemented). We hypothesize that *governance features* (as seen in the gray box at top of Figure 2.1)—the centralization, alignment, size, and resources of the separate systems—influence the feasibility of cross-system collaboration. In terms of governance structures, we understand *centralization* as referring to the hierarchical level that has authority to make decisions, take action, and allocate funding (e.g., the level of government that is responsible for managing budgets and providing services) (Hage and Aiken, 1967; Simon, 1960). *Alignment* describes the extent to which the two systems exhibit parallel

FIGURE 2.1

Conceptual Framework for Cross-System Collaboration

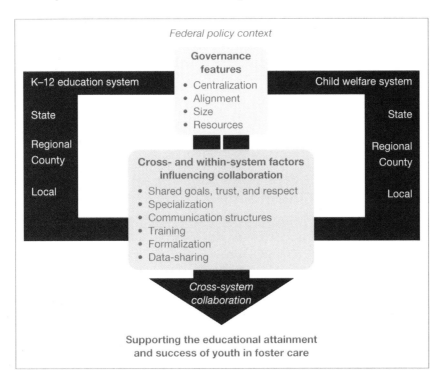

Federal policy context

Governance features
- Centralization
- Alignment
- Size
- Resources

K–12 education system

State

Regional

County

Local

Child welfare system

State

Regional

County

Local

Cross- and within-system factors influencing collaboration
- Shared goals, trust, and respect
- Specialization
- Communication structures
- Training
- Formalization
- Data-sharing

Cross-system collaboration

Supporting the educational attainment and success of youth in foster care

levels of centralization, such that we might expect ease in developing communication structures across parallel units of the two systems. The size of these agencies, as well as the expansiveness of resources, is likely to substantively influence their ability to coordinate services and create opportunities for communication.

The lower box of Figure 2.1 details the cross- and within-system factors that we might expect to influence the level of collaboration between education and child welfare systems, drawing on common factors across the extant literature on within-system collaboration. First, collaboration may be enhanced by strong relationships. Factors that contribute to good relationships are *shared goals, trust,* and *respect* (Bronstein, 2003; Herbert et al., 2021). An example of shared goals in this case might be shared views about what youth in foster care need (Stone, D'andrade, and Austin, 2007). *Trust* and *respect* between agencies and their agents appear to facilitate collaboration across organizational boundaries (Bardach, 1996; Herbert et al., 2021). We also considered the *specialization* of the workforce in both systems, specifically the experiences, roles, and responsibilities of those who serve as liaisons between the two systems (Herbert et al., 2021).

We also consider the factors that may facilitate collaboration. *Communication structures* and norms (i.e., formal and informal guidelines for appropriate communications) can allow agencies the space and content for collaboration (Stone, D'andrade, and Austin, 2007; Herbert et al., 2021). *Training*, including the extent to which it addresses the shared work of the two systems and whether it engages agents from both systems, can play a key function in linking that work (Bronstein, 2003; Herbert et al., 2021). Shared work processes might also be formalized through tools, protocols, or case review procedures to differing extents across agencies (Bronstein, 2003; Stone, D'andrade, and Austin, 2007; Herbert et al., 2021). *Formalization* of this work may present consistent opportunities and routines for collaboration. Additionally, *data-sharing* across systems and agencies is a necessary precondition for cooperative work (Stone, D'andrade, and Austin, 2007; Herbert et al., 2021).

All of these elements can also present opportunities for feedback, evaluation, and reflection that may help promote ongoing collaboration (Herbert et al., 2021; Bronstein, 2003). We focus attention on these features and factors as we explore how collaboration between education and child welfare systems plays out in our case study states and which factors appear to best facilitate collaboration. Our analyses examined each element of this conceptual framework.

CHAPTER 3

Federal Legislation Shapes Efforts at the State and Local Levels to Support the Special Student Population Served by Both Systems

Three federal laws influence the policy context related to educational outcomes for the youth served by both the education and child welfare systems: ESSA (Pub. L. 114-95, 2015), the McKinney-Vento Homeless Assistance Act (Pub. L. 100-77, 1987), and the Fostering Connections to Success and Increasing Adoptions Act (Pub. L. 110-351, 2008). ESSA reauthorized the Elementary and Secondary Education Act (ESEA) (Pub. L. 89-10, 1965), which established a significant role for the federal government in public K–12 education centered on promoting equal opportunity among all students.

Title I, Part A, of ESSA provides a mechanism for the federal government to funnel funding to state education agencies (SEAs) to support local education agencies (LEAs),[1] which we refer to in this report as *school districts*, that serve high-poverty families and provide supports for disadvantaged and low-performing students. Students who are in out-of-home care (foster family care but not group homes or residential treatment centers)[2]

---

[1] LEAs include "public charter schools that are established as an LEA under state law" (Code of Federal Regulations, Title 34, Part 303).

[2] "The requirements for ensuring educational stability for children in foster care under Section 1111(g)(1)€ apply to all children in foster care enrolled in schools in the SEA," including charter schools (U.S. Department of Education and U.S. Department of Health and Human Services, 2016, p. 6). Charter schools must follow the requirements

and those who are experiencing homelessness are eligible for services under Title I, Part A. ESSA added provisions related to youth in foster care aimed at improving education stability and collaboration between child welfare and education agencies (U.S. Department of Education and U.S. Department of Health and Human Services, 2016, pp. 6–8).[3]

ESSA's educational stability provisions complement those within Fostering Connections, which require assurances that child welfare agencies make a plan to ensure educational stability through efforts such as considering the appropriateness of the child's current school and immediate enrollment to another school if the current school is not in the best interest of the child (U.S. Department of Education and U.S. Department of Health and Human Services, 2016, pp. 4–5). ESSA also established a requirement for SEAs to report high school graduation rates, student achievement scores, and at least one other education-related indicator from the state education data system disaggregated by foster care status (Pub. L. 114-95, 2015). Additionally, ESSA amended and reauthorized McKinney-Vento, which strives to address the unique challenges of a specific student population: youth experiencing homelessness, which, as part of a previous version, included youth awaiting foster care placement.[4]

---

for a school or LEA depending on the school's charter. Although charter schools are covered by the requirement, research has highlighted the challenges that students in foster care face in accessing charter schools and other schools of choice (Trinidad and Korman, 2020). The laws do not apply to private schools.

[3] The latter served to reinforce a requirement of Fostering Connections that local child welfare agencies prioritize school stability for children placed in foster care by giving children the opportunity to remain in their original school. For more-detailed information, please see U.S. Department of Education and U.S. Department of Health and Human Services, 2016; and Legal Center for Foster Care and Education, 2016, for a summary of the joint guidance.

[4] Children and youth experiencing homelessness are defined in the legislation as those "who lack a fixed, regular, and adequate nighttime residence" (U.S. Department of Education, 2017, p. 7). Under the provisions of ESSA, students "awaiting foster care placement," who had previously been covered under McKinney-Vento in some states, are no longer eligible for the rights and benefits outlined under McKinney-Vento because these students lack a fixed residence while awaiting placement and are instead covered by the foster care provisions of ESSA (U.S. Department of Education, 2017, p. 2).

These federal laws prioritize *school stability* and give students in foster care and those experiencing homelessness the right to continued enrollment in their school of origin.[5] An alternative school placement is allowed if recommended by a process called the *best interest determination*.[6] According to these laws, school districts must immediately enroll students who are in foster care or experiencing homelessness in a new school when deemed necessary by the best interest determination, whether the student has access to their school records or not.

Two of the laws, ESSA and McKinney-Vento, actively promote cross-system collaboration among the key players: child welfare agencies, SEAs, and school districts. Table 3.1 summarizes some key differences between ESSA provisions related to youth in foster care and McKinney-Vento provisions related to youth experiencing homelessness. Below, we briefly summarize some key features of the laws relevant to cross-system collaboration and highlight how McKinney-Vento legislation and related guidance have been more detailed than ESSA in specifying process requirements at the state and local levels.

Collaboration to Promote Education Stability

ESSA and McKinney-Vento call for states to establish clear processes for school districts to follow, in collaboration with child welfare agencies for

---

[5] For a young person in foster care, the school of origin is the school at which they were enrolled at the time of foster care placement or when their foster care placement changed (U.S. Department of Education and U.S. Department of Health and Human Services, 2016, p. 11; Pub. L. 89-10, 1965, Section 1111[g][1][I][i]). For students experiencing homelessness, the school of origin is the school they were attending when they transitioned into homelessness (U.S. Department of Education, 2017, p. 23; Pub. L. 100-77, 1987, Section 722[g][3][I][i]).

[6] The definition of a *best interest determination* varies widely. Overall, the guiding principles include the young person's current circumstances, with an emphasis on their safety and well-being; other considerations include but are not limited to the parent or caregiver's capacity to provide for the young person's needs (e.g., home, food, shelter) and factors related to permanency (Child Welfare Information Gateway, 2020). This determination should be done in collaboration with individuals who are involved with the child (i.e., foster parent or biological parent), the child (if age appropriate), child welfare agency, and school staff. Ultimately, this leads to a decision about whether a school change is appropriate or not.

TABLE 3.1

Collaboration and Funding Related Provisions of ESSA and McKinney-Vento

	ESSA	McKinney-Vento
Best interest determination	• ESSA requires collaboration among child welfare agencies, SEAs, and school districts. • Non-regulatory guidance encourages development of dispute resolution and offers suggestions regarding those procedures.	• McKinney-Vento prioritizes the wishes of a parent or guardian. • McKinney-Vento requires states to have a dispute resolution mechanism regarding placement or eligibility.
Collaboration structures	• ESSA requires each state to appoint a foster care point of contact (POC) (different from the McKinney-Vento state coordinator). • ESSA encourages districts and child welfare agencies to appoint a liaison, with one exception: If child welfare appoints a POC in writing, then districts are required to appoint a POC as well. • Non-regulatory guidance encourages districts to designate a POC. • Non-regulatory guidance outlines potential roles for foster care liaisons.	• McKinney-Vento requires each state to have a state coordinator. • McKinney-Vento requires each district to have a homeless liaison. • McKinney-Vento specifies the primary job responsibilities for the state and district roles. • Non-regulatory guidance provides states with an outline of monitoring processes that districts and their corresponding liaisons must abide by.
Transportation	• ESSA requires districts receiving Title I funds to collaborate with local or state child welfare agencies to create transportation procedures.	• McKinney-Vento requires that states and districts have transportation policies. • McKinney-Vento stipulates some characteristics for those policies, including cost-sharing arrangements.

Table 3.1—Continued

	ESSA	McKinney-Vento
Funding	• Districts may use Title I, Part A, and child welfare agencies may use Title IV, Part E (Pub. L. 74-271, 1935), funds.	• Mandatory allocations of federal funds are provided to states (on the basis of the state's proportion of Title I, Part A, funding) and districts to support transportation costs and other expenses associated with aiding youth experiencing homelessness. • Districts may also apply for competitive subgrant opportunities available to districts servicing youth experiencing homelessness.

SOURCES: Derived from Pub. L. 114-95, 2015; Pub. L. 100-77, 1987.

those children who are involved in the child welfare system, when considering a placement other than the school of origin (McNaught and Peeler, 2017). The two laws specify slightly different processes for that best interest determination. ESSA requires that child welfare agencies, the SEA, and school districts collaborate in making a best interest determination regarding students in foster care. Non-regulatory guidance encourages the development of dispute resolution procedures and suggests that, when disputes cannot be resolved, child welfare agencies should "be considered the final decision maker . . . unless State law or policy dictates otherwise" (U.S. Department of Education and U.S. Department of Health and Human Services, 2016, p. 14). In contrast, McKinney-Vento is more directive regarding students experiencing homelessness: The law prioritizes the wishes of the parent or guardian in determining the best interest of the child. McKinney-Vento also requires each state plan to have dispute resolution mechanisms and provides joint guidance on decisionmaking when a dispute emerges between involved parties regarding placement or eligibility (U.S. Department of Education, 2017, p. 32; Pub. L. 100-77, Section 722[g][1][C]). Notably, although the preferences of the youth should be considered, their participation in these deliberations is not required by either of these laws.

Structures for Collaboration and Accountability

Both laws promote collaboration between the child welfare and education systems by requiring or recommending certain roles within each system. McKinney-Vento requires that each state have a state coordinator for homeless education (state coordinator), and that each school district have a homeless education liaison. States must post information about the liaisons on the SEA website and update that information annually. McKinney-Vento specifies the primary job responsibilities for state coordinators and local liaisons, as well as the skills of the individuals holding the position. Notably, the state coordinators are required to offer professional development for the local liaisons as well as other school district staff and to monitor the local liaisons to ensure compliance with McKinney-Vento (U.S. Department of Education, 2017, p. 12).

ESSA requires that states appoint a foster care liaison, who must be different from the McKinney-Vento coordinator.[7] ESSA encourages school districts and child welfare agencies to appoint such a liaison as well, but it is not required in all instances.[8] However, non-regulatory guidance encourages the LEA to designate a POC and to consider whether the chosen individual has the capacity and resources needed to carry out their duties, thereby expanding on statutory requirements (U.S. Department of Education, 2017, p. 21). Federal guidance outlines potential roles and responsibilities for foster care liaisons but gives states flexibility to develop their own guidance. ESSA requires the SEA to "conduct regular monitoring and oversight to guarantee appropriate implementation of these provisions at a local level," yet there is no additional guidance on how the state should accomplish this oversight (U.S. Department of Education, 2017, p. 7). ESSA encourages but

---

[7] The foster care liaison is referred to as the state foster care POC by the U.S. Department of Education.

[8] There is one exception to this: If the child welfare agencies established a liaison and notifies the LEA in writing, the LEA must appoint a POC (Pub. L. 89-10, 1965, Section 1112[c][5][A]).

does not require child welfare agencies to appoint a foster care liaison on educational matters, although there is guidance to assist in developing roles and responsibilities for such a role once established. Regardless of whether a state has established a formal child welfare system liaison, collaboration between the education system and child welfare system is required under federal law (U.S. Department of Education and U.S. Department of Health and Human Services, 2016, p. 21).

Collaboration on Transportation

Students in foster care or who are experiencing homelessness are entitled by law to transportation to and from their school of origin when continued enrollment is deemed to be in the student's best interest. For example, McKinney-Vento requires that SEAs and school districts have transportation policies and procedures and stipulates some characteristics for those policies and procedures, such as in cases when students move from one school district to another (U.S. Department of Education, 2017, p. 27). This law specifies that if a student experiencing homelessness moves to a neighboring school district, the two districts must share the transportation costs equally unless they come to another mutual agreement (Pub. L. 100-77, 1987, Section 722[g][1][J][iii][I]).

ESSA requires districts to collaborate with local or state child welfare agencies to create written transportation procedures to ensure that students in foster care have access to their school of origin but does not specify which entity (one or both districts or the local child welfare agency) is responsible for covering the additional costs of such transportation (Pub. L. 114-95, 2015, Section 1112[c][5][B]). Some states specify cost-sharing expectations, while others give flexibility to school districts. Many agreements, typically in the form of memoranda of understanding (MOUs), are district-specific and vary widely (McNaught and Peeler, 2017).

Collaboration on Funding

Both education and child welfare services for students in foster care and children who are experiencing homelessness are supported by funding at the federal, state, and local levels. In terms of education services, both school districts and child welfare agencies can fund transportation services for students in foster care who are eligible for Social Security Administration payments through Title IV, Part E funds,[9] which constitute the major federal funding used by child welfare agencies (Social Security Administration, undated). However, not all youth in foster care are eligible for these funds.[10] McKinney-Vento provides federal funds to SEAs and LEAs to support educational stability and success, including transportation costs. These funds are distributed across states in the same proportion as Title I, Part A, allocations. States must allocate at least three-quarters of the funding provided to school districts through subgrants. However, although a majority of school districts receive at least some Title I, Part A, funding (Snyder et al., 2019), roughly one-quarter of districts receive McKinney-Vento allocations (National Center for Homeless Education, 2019). This overview reveals the complexity and local nature of the funding implications that follow from a best interest determination. Therefore, it is not surprising that disputes arise during this process.

Additionally, both ESSA and McKinney-Vento allow SEAs and school districts to use, at their discretion, federal education funding provided under Title I, Part A (focused on helping high-need students);[11] Title II, Part A (focused on instruction); and Title IV, Part A (focused on capacity), to fund supports for students in foster care and students experiencing homelessness. However, given the scope of activities and student populations that may be supported by the sources, leveraging them to support students in foster care and students experiencing homelessness involves trade-offs between spending on these groups and other student populations. In addition to the allocated McKinney-Vento funds, school districts serving youth experiencing

---

[9] Under Section 475(4)(A) of the Social Security Act (Pub. L. 74-271, 1935) youth in foster care may be eligible to receive "foster care maintenance payments." These payments can be used by a Title IV, Part E agency serving the child to cover a range of expenses, including transportation to the school of origin (U.S. Department of Education, 2017, p. 27).

[10] During fiscal year (FY) 2020, only 39 percent of youth in foster care were eligible for this funding (Sciamanna, undated).

[11] Notably, funds that are "reserved for comparable services for homeless children and youth under section 1113(c)(3)(A)(i) of the ESEA may not be used to provide transportation needed to maintain children in foster care in their schools of origin" (U.S. Department of Education, 2017, p. 19; Pub. L. 89-10, 1965).

homelessness can apply for competitive grants to cover expenditures associated with these laws. These are not guaranteed and are awarded based on the need of the school district and application quality (Pub. L. 100-77, 1987, Section 723[c]). Although there is federal education funding available, some have described ESSA's foster care provisions as an unfunded mandate (Klein and Ujifusa, 2016; Stringer, 2018) because of the lack of targeted funding available to support the services detailed in ESSA as it relates to students in foster care.

CHAPTER 4

Findings

States Differ in How They Govern Education and Child Welfare Systems

Within the confines of federal policy, we found substantial variation in how states govern education and child welfare systems. We compiled information about governance structure for both systems for the United States—all states, territories, and the District of Columbia—to identify potential indicators that could characterize the governance features and factors likely to influence cross-system collaboration highlighted in Figure 2.1. The sources we reviewed and the indicators we developed are specified in the appendix. We used these indicators to inform the selection of states, counties, and districts for the case studies.

We found publicly available information for each state addressing several areas, as summarized in Table 4.1. We used data on system centralization to consider alignment, as described below.

In addition, we reviewed the availability of child welfare and educational outcomes for each state. We found that state policies in defining foster care and various elements of a young person's transitions vary across states and even across agencies within a state.

Centralization and Fragmentation Within Child Welfare and Education Systems

To address the degree of centralization of governance, we considered the level of governance (state, county, or local) at which authority to make decisions, take action, and allocate funding is concentrated for each system. To consider fragmentation, we developed metrics at the state, district, and

TABLE 4.1

Publicly Available State-by-State Data Used in Governance Analysis

	Education	Child Welfare
Centralization	• How state legislation or constitution assigns responsibility for education services within the state • Dedicated state-level capacity for collaboration among early care and K–12 education systems • Powers and duties of the state board of education • Number of counties, operational districts, and operational schools • Ratio of district to county and schools to districts • Independent and dependent school district governments	• Governance hierarchy
Size	• Enrollment (K–12 and prekindergarten) • Average population per school district	• Number of children in foster care in the fiscal year • Number of children entering foster care • Maltreatment victim rate per 1,000 children
Resources	• Total funding, revenue, and spending • Revenue (total, state, and local) • Average spent per pupil	• Total federal, state, and local expenditures

county levels to gauge the relative size of each system, the number of individuals served, and corresponding resource needs at each level (see the appendix). For each state, we computed a ratio of the number of districts to the number of counties as an indicator of the governance complexity or fragmentation for education systems. For example, Hawaii, the only state to be governed at the state level within both the child welfare and education systems and the only state to have only one school district, has a ratio of districts to counties that is well below one district per county. At the other end of the spectrum, Arizona has a ratio of about 48 districts per county, while the average across the United States and the District of Columbia is about ten districts per county, suggesting that fragmentation of the education systems varies substantially across the states.

Alignment of Governance Across Systems

To summarize the degree of alignment of governance across systems—
or the extent to which education and child welfare systems exhibit parallel levels of centralization—we developed a matrix that categorized states
based on the degree of centralization of its education and child welfare systems. Table 4.2 summarizes our simplified observations. The vast majority
of state education systems are administered at the county (27 percent) or
local level (70 percent). In contrast, 78 percent of state child welfare systems are state-administered, and 18 percent are county-administered. None

TABLE 4.2

Comparison of Systems Governance for All States and District of Columbia

	Education System		
Child Welfare System	State	County	Local
State-Administered	Hawaii	Alabama, Arkansas, Florida, Georgia, Kentucky, Maryland, Mississippi, South Carolina, Tennessee, West Virginia, Wyoming	Alaska, Arizona, Connecticut, Delaware, District of Columbia, Idaho, Illinois, Indiana, Iowa, Kansas, Louisiana, Maine, Massachusetts, Michigan, Missouri, Montana, Nebraska, New Hampshire, New Jersey, New Mexico, Oklahoma, Oregon, Rhode Island, South Dakota, Texas, Utah, Vermont, Washington
County-Administered		North Carolina, Virginia	California, Colorado, Minnesota, New York, North Dakota, Ohio, Pennsylvania
Hybrid		Nevada	Wisconsin

is administered locally.[1] Just a few states (Hawaii, North Carolina, Virginia, and Nevada) have systems that appear to use identical governance organizations for both child welfare and education systems.

Size and Resources

We examined total state expenditures per student in foster care, by state, to shed light on child welfare system size and resources (Rosinsky et al., 2021; Children's Bureau, 2021; Child Trends, 2021). Variation in this metric across states was large (see Table 4.3). The highest-spending state (New Jersey) spent 29 times more per youth in foster care in 2018 than the lowest-spending state (Wyoming). Child welfare agencies typically use about half of all their funding (federal, state, and local) to cover out-of-home placement (45 percent), followed by adoption and guardianship (19 percent) (Rosinsky et al., 2021).

For the education system, we looked at average per pupil spending by state (Hanson, 2022; National Center for Education Statistics, 2022b). Variation in per-pupil expenditures by state is much smaller than it is for the child welfare system. The highest-spending state (New York) spent three times more per pupil in 2018 than the lowest-spending state (Utah). To understand the relative magnitude of funding each system possesses to serve its target population and the variation across states, we also looked at the ratio of state expenditures for child welfare per youth in foster care and education expenditures per student. On average, total child welfare expenditures are about 25 percent of the total education expenditures (Rosinsky et al., 2021). But this percentage varies dramatically by state, with a nine-fold difference between the state with the highest percentage (Connecticut) and the lowest (Delaware).

We also examined the relative size of each system by comparing the size of the state's population of youth in foster care in FY 2020 with school-age children as measured by K–12 system enrollment. Because some youth in

---

[1] There are limited data available regarding governance metrics for U.S. territories, except Puerto Rico. Puerto Rico is state-administered and is considered a state for the purposes of Title IV, Part B and Title IV, Part E of the Social Security Act (Pub. L. 74-271, 1935) (Child Welfare Information Gateway, 2018).

TABLE 4.3

Relative Variation Within State-Level Systems

	Child Welfare		Education
	Total Expenditure per Youth in Foster Care in FY 2018	Ratio of Number of Children in Foster Care to Total Enrolled in K–12	Average Spent per Pupil
Minimum	$10,362 (Wyoming)	0.3 (New Jersey)	$7,478 (Utah)
Average (all states, District of Columbia, and Puerto Rico)	$77,112.52	0.9	$12,953.35
Maximum	$297,674 (New Jersey)	2.7 (West Virginia)	$23,321 (New York)
California	$92,997	0.8	$12,728
Georgia	$63,788	0.6	$10,769
Washington	$53,220	0.9	$12,830
Wisconsin	$63,812	0.8	$12,466

SOURCES: Child Trends, 2021; Child Welfare Information Gateway, 2021; National Center for Education Statistics, 2020; Hanson, 2022.

foster care do not fall within the K–12 age range, this metric should not be interpreted to reflect the share of the school-age population in the foster care system. On average, youth in foster care make up just under 1 percent of the student population in the education system.

Collaboration Indicators in Education and Child Welfare Systems

To further explore the landscape of state governance features, we considered a range of potential cross-system collaboration indicators in these systems. We were able to gather systematic data across states for the indicators listed below (see the appendix for more detail). Our review of these indicators showed substantial variation in types of collaboration across the states.

For example, our review of the extant sources described above revealed the following:

- Five states had denoted students in foster care as a specific subgroup within their school accountability systems (Education Commission of the States, 2021b).
- Two states and the District of Columbia had allotted supplemental funding for students in foster care (Education Commission of the States, 2021a).
- Twenty-four states and the District of Columbia could link prekindergarten and K–12 data with foster care data (Data Quality Campaign, 2016).
- Eighteen states and the District of Columbia had legislation predating ESSA that touched on education stability or continuity, five had legislation that discussed information-sharing, and six addressed interagency collaboration (National Conferences of State Legislatures, 2016).
- Nine states had current or previous interagency or MOU agreements on file (Legal Center for Foster Care and Education, undated).

On the whole, we found wide variation in how education and child welfare systems are organized and operate across the states despite the foundation of federal legislation. Indeed, gathering comparable state-specific information about each system proved to be a significant undertaking in itself, demonstrating the challenges in understanding the complexity of cross-system collaboration. Next, we explore this variation through case studies of states purposefully selected to represent variation across these governance features.

Case Data Indicate That Several Factors Contributed to and Inhibited Collaboration

Our case studies demonstrated that cross-system collaboration is both a goal and a challenge for education and child welfare systems.

> ## Case Study Design
>
> - We selected four states for data collection: California, Georgia, Washington, and Wisconsin.
> - The states reflected variation in size, centralization, fragmentation, and alignment.
> - We selected nested counties and districts to represent metro and nonmetro settings.
> - We conducted interviews with administrators in education and child welfare agencies at the state level ($n = 7$ participants) and at the regional, county, or district levels ($n = 7$ participants). All participants served the needs of youth in foster care as part of their roles and responsibilities in their agencies.
> - We conducted group interviews with 12 adults who had previously experienced foster care in these case states.

Some common enabling factors emerged across these case study states, such as specialized liaison roles across system levels, communication structures to foster cross-system social engagement at the state and local levels, codification of collaboration in legislation and procedure, and data- and other information-sharing across agencies. Common challenges also emerged, including divergent system goals, high levels of staff turnover, inadequate training, and geographic dispersion that constrained the ability of systems to maintain school stability and support services. Adults who have experienced foster care—those most affected by lack of collaboration—affirmed these common challenges and enabling factors, and recommended changes to improve cross-system collaboration at the case level.

Adults Who Have Experienced Foster Care Noted the Importance of Student and Caregiver Voices, a Caring Point of Contact at School, and a Connection to Resources

Before reviewing the system-level findings, we highlight critical factors that could support improved educational outcomes as articulated by those directly affected by the education and child welfare systems. The adults who have experienced foster care with whom we spoke described highly varied circumstances leading to their entrance into foster care. Our sample included individuals who had initially entered foster care between the ages of three and 16, whose placements included time spent in foster care, group homes, kinship care, and transitional living. Their school stability experience ranged from no school changes to around 15 school changes (with an average of four school changes). They experienced changes in caseworker assignments ranging from a single caseworker to six caseworkers over the course of their interaction with the foster care system. Almost half of our respondents had attended both traditional, comprehensive schools and nontraditional schools—continuation high schools, a private Catholic school, juvenile court schools, virtual charter schools, and homeschooling. In practice, students appreciated alternative placements during certain periods of their education, but most noted that they benefited from graduating from comprehensive high schools.

Across these respondents, common challenges arose because of changes in caseworker support or policy. Some respondents described having to change schools when their caseworker changed. For example, one adult who has experienced foster care had a one-hour commute, driven to school by their caseworker. When the caseworker changed, the young person's school assignment also changed to a school closer to the foster home. Three-quarters of the respondents reported that they were not provided the opportunity to offer their opinion on their school of choice during placement changes.

Respondents' experiences of school stability decisionmaking also highlighted the complexity of determining a student's best interest. For example, one respondent was a parenting student and had attended an alternative school that provided a flexible schedule and child care for the student's infant, which they found very useful. With a change in caseworker, and the encouragement of the foster parents, this respondent was placed back at a comprehensive school despite their own desire to remain at the alternative site. As the respondent explained:

> Honestly at the time I was upset because . . . at that [prior alternative] school I was able to take my son with me . . . and the teachers will assist

you with the children . . . . But I graduated from a regular high school and I liked it better now, in the long run . . . [because] I was able to do a lot more stuff.

However, this respondent also stated that the choice of schools was particularly helpful because their foster parent was a teacher at the comprehensive high school and therefore able to support her studies. When asked what helped them to get on track to graduate from high school and go to college, this student shared:

When my son turned about like nine months, I went to the regular high school in that town, and she [my foster parent] was very on top of me about my homework and my grades. But I mean, it could also be because she was a teacher at school.

This perspective demonstrates how youth voices, along with the involvement of families and a stable caseworker, are a crucial component of the best interest determination to ensure that placements fit the needs of the student. Negotiating the interests and needs of youth and their supporters can help to identify the best placement.

Almost all respondents noted that there were delays in transferring their school records and beginning classes after a school change, ranging from two to six weeks of lost instructional time. School supports for youth in foster care also varied substantially; some respondents had no dedicated POC, while others received therapeutic support groups. In practice, however, almost all respondents reported that they felt that the stigma of being identified as someone in foster care held them back from participating in and using these services.

The young people we spoke to also offered recommendations for improving the support for the education of youth in foster care. Two-thirds of our respondents noted the importance of therapeutic counseling services on their school campus, available as needed. One-third also noted that youth in foster care would benefit if educators and school leads had broader training on trauma-informed care to better support and advocate for the needs of youth who had experienced trauma preceding or following their foster care placement.

Half of our respondents said that youth in foster care need one POC at school (i.e., someone who can serve as a supporter and counselor to youth outside their academics). Respondents discussed the need for someone on campus to check in with students in foster care about their well-being and provide positive feedback when students are doing well (as opposed to receiving an intervention only if they were failing classes, for example). One-third of our respondents also noted that a quiet, private space on campus would be helpful to youth in foster care, who might need a peaceful space to self-regulate or do homework.

Furthermore, more than half of our respondents noted that it would be helpful to have some additional support in preparing for independent living (e.g., budgeting, applying for resources or supports) to help with their transitions to college and careers. A few respondents had, in fact, benefited substantially from independent living or transitional housing services in cases where they turned 18 prior to their high school graduation. In some cases, these programs were able to assist youth with transportation to school or work and provide other support services. Nonetheless, our respondents noted that additional supports and information about existing resources could be very helpful in managing this transition. Most respondents described how challenging it could be to even apply for the resources already available to them as youth currently or formerly in foster care, such as subsidized child care, health insurance, and free computing hardware. Respondents recommended that support in identifying and applying for existing resources be provided to youth in later stages of high school and after age 18.

Regional Governance Was Not Well Aligned Across Systems

In each of our four state case studies, child welfare agencies were organized at the state and regional (or county, in the case of California and Georgia) levels. In some cases, contractors assist with placement services. Education agencies are organized at the state, regional (or county, in the case of California and Wisconsin), and local district levels. Interestingly, in two cases, the regional designations on the education and child welfare systems are not aligned. That is, the regions used in the two systems are not analogous. As a result, collaborative arrangements often span different levels and geographic regions to cooperatively support the education of youth in foster care.

Agencies Collaborated on School Stability, Transportation, and Support Services

Education and child welfare agencies in these case study states generally collaborated in three common areas: placement decisions and school stability, transportation agreements and cost-sharing, and case management and support. As youth enter foster care, change placements, or return to parents, they often move across school or district enrollment boundaries.

The states varied in their approach to implementing federal policy to promote school stability, as described above. For example, motivated by the stipulations of ESSA, as well as a state assembly bill (AB) on continuity and permanence in care (AB 403; see California State Assembly, 2015), California has implemented a best-interest-determination process that integrates the preferences of the student, the student's parent or education decision-maker, the student's attachment to the school (including peers and staff), sibling placement, school climate, history of school transfers, Individualized Education Plan (IEP) and English-language-learner services, and length of commute. Educational liaisons had responsibility for supporting appropriate educational placements. In Washington, caseworkers, caregivers, and school or district representatives had opportunities to meet and discuss placement using a similar set of criteria.

Changes to placement combined with stability of schooling often resulted in the need for additional transportation services to assist students in commuting to and from school, often across district or even county lines. Our case study states have taken differing approaches to collaboration on ESSA-mandated transportation provisions. California requires written policies on transportation, but such agreements varied substantially. Some states rely on guidance from state transportation MOUs, yet not all states have this guidance available. Across all four states, MOUs were in place to delineate which agencies were responsible for specific costs associated with such transportation services. In two of our cases, child welfare liaisons at the state or regional level were assigned to process all reimbursement requests and manage jurisdictional disagreements. Despite these coordination efforts, respondents in all states reported that arranging the logistics of transportation at the local level remained a challenge. One state-level respondent noted how transportation provisions are easier to access in urban areas than rural areas. In the words of this leader,

> There are definitely, at the county level, a lot of different examples and variations of the cost-sharing and the responsibility sharing. Everything from districts being reimbursed by the child welfare authority for transportation they're doing with LEA vehicles to sharing costs for contracted transportation providers.

In one county, a foster care liaison noted that they had worked with all districts to identify countywide transportation plans to avoid coordinating with multiple district-specific MOUs and arrangements, especially as youth often had to cross district or county boundaries to attend school. Nonetheless, as noted by Burns and colleagues, a little more than half of California's counties had transportation MOUs in place by 2019, as "misaligned priorities about transportation agreements can complicate county agency collaboration" (2022, p. 20).

Finally, liaisons at the state and regional levels across all cases noted that they periodically received specific cases to coordinate services. These included examples in which youth in foster care required specialized health or behavioral services or transportation across long distances or rural areas with limited transportation services and in which disputes arose over school placement. The liaisons' involvement varied from clarifying policies and roles (e.g., who was responsible for managing behavioral issues occurring at school or which agency was responsible for transportation) to troubleshooting how to provide support services (e.g., tutoring or IEP services) in areas with limited resources.

Systems Rely on Relationships to Build Trust and Bridge Gaps Between System Goals

In all cases, respondents identified commonalities in liaisons' goals in both education and child welfare agencies. One education liaison in a state child welfare agency shared their goal:

The education stability. I think it's the mobility of moving around. I think that is one of the biggest risks that the child welfare system presents to a child. . . . And so my number one focus is to make sure that policy is clear and then social workers and school have the information they need and primarily my people, who are social workers . . . know to do the best interest determination.

For those not in liaison roles, however, the goal of education stability is often weighed against other priorities. Across states, respondents consistently reiterated that the primary concern of caseworkers is child safety, which necessarily comes before educational stability. In the words of one education liaison in a regional child welfare office:

We want what's best for kids, we want them to be educated, so I think it pretty much lines up [with the focus of education personnel]. I think for school folks, the top priority is education because that's what they do, that's their role. And for us, education may feel like sometimes it's not our top priority because, you know, [our top priority], it's child safety. It's very important to us and we continue to educate about how important school stability is, and kids lose six months every time they move schools, and keep them in the school of origin and here's why we do it, and those kinds of issues. It's just continuing to educate folks [caseworkers].

As this quotation demonstrates, liaisons in both education and child welfare play an important bridging role, overcoming organizational, spatial, and social boundaries to pursue a shared goal of school stability amid other pressing concerns.

The tensions between these varied goals and priorities of education and child welfare appeared to influence the level of trust and respect between agencies. Liaisons in about half of our states described very close working relationships with their counterparts and described strong trust and respect. In general, however, concerns arose over whether educational stability would be prioritized by child welfare agencies and caseworkers. One foster care liaison in an education agency described this tension as follows:

I think part of it is just human nature. If people don't really understand what the other person's roles and responsibilities are, they don't know how to manage their expectations. . . . [Educational stability] might be on the radar for the schools, but ultimately it would be child welfare who decides whether or not to put the child into foster care. Ideally, all of those child welfare workers would know the law, would know that those kids are entitled to stay in their school of origin. . . . But most social workers don't know what the best interest determination is; they aren't familiar with the law; they don't know that the school has foster care liaisons; they don't know that the school provides transportation; and often they don't communicate to the school that a child has been placed in foster care.

In the view of this respondent, despite strong trust among state and regional representatives across the two systems, trust remained low in the understanding and commitment of those working directly with youth on the ground.

In some states, nonprofits or community-based organizations fulfilled an important bridging role, which varied from engaging in statewide task forces to providing additional support in case management. This often involved reaching out to the appropriate education liaisons, school staff, and caseworkers to ensure that youth were provided appropriate resources and supports. In at least one case in which a nonprofit was contracted for this purpose, this role was viewed as highly beneficial to cross-system communication.

Cross-System Liaisons Helped Elevate the Importance of Education-Related Outcomes

We examined the specialization of roles and responsibilities, particularly of those who were tasked with bridging the boundaries and promoting collaboration between education and child welfare agencies. Across our cases, education agencies generally designated state and district liaisons, with California and Wisconsin also housing county- or regional-level liaisons to foster care. In Washington, since 2018, legislation mandates the identification of foster care POCs in each school building (Revised Code of Washington, 2018). In contrast, child welfare agencies only had state education liaisons in California and Washington, while Washington also designated regional education liaisons within child welfare. On the whole, it appeared that education agencies were better positioned than child welfare agencies to designate specific services for their population of youth in foster care. These liaisons played a crucial role in translating the policies across agencies, as one child welfare regional liaison shared:

> The language, acronyms, those kinds of things are definitely something we work on every day because what . . . this means to us [child welfare], what it means to them [education], and just clarifying those and communicating and having that person to translate is invaluable.

Liaisons in both education and child welfare often held more than one role. In child welfare agencies, education liaisons often also held other roles, such as coordinating child records. In education, across levels, foster care liaisons often also held responsibilities for McKinney-Vento services for students experiencing homelessness or migrant education. Foster care was more often combined with several other roles at more-local levels (e.g., districts and schools). Of note, a few respondents identified characteristics of these roles that facilitated liaison work at the district level, noting that it was important for these liaisons to hold enough authority in their roles (e.g., as principals or school counselors) to advocate for youth. In addition, a few respondents noted that sharing McKinney-Vento responsibilities with foster care oversight generally worked well, as policies governing the educational rights of these two populations were somewhat similar.

Communication Was Intentionally Structured to Promote Networking and Common Understanding

Across cases, liaisons sought to develop structured opportunities for communication across the child welfare and education systems. In all cases, state agencies in particular participated in a variety of cross-functional meetings. In California, for example, foster care liaisons at the state education agency described meeting "five to six times a month" with child welfare representatives in various councils, committees, and advisories, including the Foster Youth Services Coordinating Programs, executive advisory councils, and various task forces. A county educational liaison, too, mentioned collaborating with child welfare representatives through the California Foster Youth Education Task Force, Improving Educational Outcomes for Children in Care Conference, Child Welfare and Attendance meetings, and the Foster Care Advisory Council. While well-developed in California, these structured, regular collaborative meetings across education and welfare were common in all cases, sometimes codified through legislation (as in Washington).

At the regional and local levels, some states used meet-and-greet opportunities to allow regional agency staff, district liaisons, and caseworkers to get to know one another and learn a bit about each other's services. Although a basic overview of policies and procedure was sometimes provided, the primary aim of these meetings was to promote social connections. One regional child welfare liaison described the benefits of these meetings:

> We [at the regional child welfare agency] are in frequent communication with those professionals [district liaisons], and our region has held what we call "coffee breaks," which we would show up at a regional office with coffee and treats and have invited the liaisons in that county and social workers to talk about "this is what my job is" and "this is what my job is" and "this is how we interface," which was often revelatory because we didn't understand each other very well. It also provided a foundation to build relationships, so that when we hit some barriers or conflict around who's going to transport a child, or whether this child can safely come back to that school or whether getting an updated IEP was a barrier, we had a relationship and could talk face to face with people that we knew.

Essentially, these opportunities for communication among district personnel, caseworkers, and regional child welfare agencies forged social connections that proved valuable in managing conflicts and cooperating on supporting youth.

Both Systems Used Training to Build Understanding Among Staff About Policies and Roles, but the Child Welfare System Appeared to Face Greater Challenges Implementing Such Training

An important role for liaisons across the cases was to provide training and support to caseworkers and educators. These trainings varied from statewide professional development on the policies surrounding the education of youth in foster care; to regional trainings on policy implementation; to large conferences to bring together educators, caseworkers, caregivers, and youth formerly in foster care to understand the challenges in accessing adequate educational opportunities. In one state, state education representatives collaborated with regional child welfare personnel to co-train staff. As one foster care liaison in a state education agency explained:

> We do a lot of collaborative trainings where she [the education liaison at the regional child welfare office] and I will train. My favorite is when we go to a child welfare office, and we invite all the neighboring districts. We'll get ten or 15 district folks in there and the regional child welfare staff and then she and I do a training together with all of them and make them talk to each other.

Respondents noted that, for those who attended, trainings provided valuable opportunities to establish a common understanding of policy and procedure and to create social connections that help educators and caseworkers collaborate to address the particular needs of students.

Nonetheless, across our cases, respondents noted several common challenges in training caseworkers and educators. First, these trainings were not mandatory and attracted only motivated personnel. For education personnel, this often included those with more-flexible schedules (e.g., counselors, assistant principals) rather than teachers. One respondent noted the challenges that arose:

> The issue sometimes is that most of our trainings are for counselors, school administrators. We're unsure if information trickle[s] down to the classroom and the teachers, security officers, bus drivers, and those lower-level educational professionals that don't have access to our training.

Given the relatively small population of youth in foster care in districts and schools, these trainings were typically attended by dedicated liaisons rather than by general staff.

Similarly, respondents across our cases noted challenges in engaging caseworkers. Multiple respondents across almost all case states noted that caseworkers did not receive any mandatory training on education. Very high turnover rates of caseworkers meant that caseworkers often did not get a chance to attend education trainings in their short tenure, or caseworkers might leave their positions after training. The aim of these trainings, particularly in two states, focused on ensuring that caseworkers used placement procedures and appropriate forms (e.g., best-interest-determination or school notification forms) in their work.

Legislation and Formalized Routines Forged Shared Understanding

All case states drew on state legislation and routines to structure and formalize collaboration between education and child welfare. First, some states had legislation requiring collaboration, such as Washington's Project Education Impact (Washington State Legislature, 2018) and California's AB 2083 (California State Assembly, 2018). These policies require collaboration across child welfare, education, and other departments and partners. These policies uniquely create accountability for collaboration across agencies in these states. Similarly, these states also have legislation predating ESSA that extends the entitlements from McKinney-Vento to all youth in foster care, such as Washington's transportation cost-sharing policies and some entitlements within California's AB 490 (California State Assembly, 2003).

In addition, our case study states also engaged in creating policies that govern routines (e.g., best interest determination), criteria to determine care placements and school enrollment, and school notification procedures. To support the legislation and policies, all our states described using MOUs to formalize transportation agreements between districts and counties or the state. These ranged from individualized district agreements (in Washington) to county-level agreements (in California). Indeed, education on and implementation of routines, along with related forms and procedures, were major foci of communications and training efforts across all case states.

Data-Sharing Appeared to Promote Stronger Collaboration

Sharing of data between education and child welfare provided important links between the systems, allowing them to coordinate services and facili-

Codifying Best-Interest-Determination Procedure and Embedding on Forms

In Washington, child welfare and education agencies developed several procedures around placement and school stability, including a best-interest-determination process as part of a Family Group Decision Meeting, where any student moves were planned. During this process, a school notification form is generated, which would let the schools know where a child would be enrolling and whether they required nutrition services, transportation, or other supports. Interestingly, this state made the unique move of printing a best-interest-determination checklist, adapted from the "Best Practices: School Selection for Students in Out-of-Home Care" issue brief (Legal Center for Foster Care and Education and National Center for Homeless Education, 2009), on the back of the school notification. In addition, the form provided a link to a brief on best practices in school selection for youth in foster care published by the Washington Office of Superintendent of Public Instruction (undated). This ensured that all involved parties considered (and had guidance on) best practices for ensuring school stability when completing the school notification form. This was a unique method to formalize decisionmaking and promote school stability through interagency collaboration.

tate enrollment and attendance. Data-sharing across our case states ranged from more labor-intensive and less detailed to highly sophisticated. In one state, case managers gathered education records and information, which were then entered into a shared workbook within the school district. This provides information on the number of youth in foster care, their placement information, and such details as transportation needs or best interest determination. Nonetheless, education and child welfare respondents noted that additional real-time information could facilitate support for youth in foster care. As one foster care representative shared:

> Just being able to have that information exchanged between the two agencies would be really helpful for us because that would save us time and having to bug teachers to count days and have counselors, having to count days and email us back about the number of tardies

or the number of absences or how many were excused? If we could just exchange just that basic information, [if] there was an interface that would help us exchange that data. If just that IEP information was available or that I like for them to know how the kids' grades are. If we had access to their grades, so that we could talk about that when we go out to the home with the parents, see what services we can connect them to that can help with that.

In two of the case states, state legislation enabled the creation of data systems to automate information-sharing on a nightly or weekly basis. Despite the necessity of and universal support for data- and information-sharing, variation across the cases was plainly evident.

Common Challenges Included High Staff Turnover, Geographical Dispersion

The primary challenge noted by respondents across cases concerned high levels of turnover, particularly among caseworkers. Education and child welfare liaisons acknowledged the immense stress and difficulty of casework and the related low retention of caseworkers. This presented a major challenge to collaboration, as caseworkers have limited opportunities to be trained in educational stability and support.

In addition, geographic differences presented major challenges in some states. In some cases, regional centers encompass a broad area, such that a liaison might need to make a three-hour drive to meet with a district liaison regarding case management. Of course, these large distances also mean that students were sometimes subject to long commutes to maintain school stability. Limited public transportation also presented challenges in supporting students in getting to and from their assigned school. The crux of these challenges is that there are often few foster caregivers in specific rural communities, making educational stability extremely difficult to maintain.

In these states, respondents noted challenges related to the differing abilities of urban and rural areas to serve their students. In particular, rural communities often had fewer resources available. For example, one child welfare regional liaison noted that rural communities were sometimes not able to supply local providers for education-support services to which students were entitled (e.g., tutoring, counseling, specialized therapies). In one

Sharing Data and Linking Accountability and Funding in California

California's data-sharing agreements emerged from state legislation tying school funding to performance metrics, which identify youth in foster care as a target population of students. Under the Local Control Funding Formula, school districts in California are mandated to create performance plans that specify how they will use funding to support the needs of youth in foster care. The outcomes of youth in foster care are tracked and compared against the general population and other subgroups in publicly available dashboards. In addition, data on absenteeism, suspension rates, graduation rates, college-going rates, and standardized test performance at school, district, county, and state levels are publicly available, disaggregated by foster care status. Counties also receive up-to-date data on school placement on a weekly basis and, for an additional fee paid to the Sacramento County Office of Education (which developed the platform and compiles the data), can access a platform with more-detailed child welfare information linked to their students, including alerts for changes in attendance or performance.

In addition to using these data to track student placements and ensure that students are appropriately supported, state and county personnel have used these data to examine needs and bright spots for better serving youth in foster care. As one foster care liaison in education explained:

> We look in their [districts'] LCAPs [Local Control Accountability Plans]. We've done some case studies with the districts who have performed really well in certain state local indicators on the dashboard. We've had case studies, we've done webinars, we wrote that report about some of the things that these districts were implementing to that maybe related to the success of their foster youth.

In this way, the documentation, sharing, and accessibility of data provides opportunities to engage in meaningful improvement efforts.

case state, students were reportedly being diverted from suburban school districts to large urban districts because the smaller districts "wanted to get rid of them." Respondents reported that this was often the case for Black and Latinx youth in foster care and that these placements were often not in the best interest of students. Finally, interviewees mentioned challenges stemming from mobility across state lines—something that is not clearly anticipated in federal legislation. This issue of cross-state mobility was also highlighted in one report: In 2019, 100 out of 621 school-age youth in foster care in Washington, D.C., were attending school in Maryland or Virginia (Trinidad and Korman, 2020, p. 15).

CHAPTER 5

Policy Considerations and Directions for Future Research

This study sought to understand the landscape of collaboration between education and child welfare systems across the nation, along with common enabling and constraining factors and promising practices. Because these analyses are primarily descriptive and exploratory, we suggest several policy considerations at the local, state, and federal levels, as well as directions for future research on this important topic.

Policy Considerations

Local Level

The local level—school district– and county-level child welfare agency in states with decentralized child welfare systems—is where the results of system collaboration (or lack thereof) have direct, practical implications for youth in foster care and those who directly interact with them. There appear to be ample opportunities to promote collaboration between education and child welfare systems to better support students at the local level through both local and regional efforts. Our policy considerations at the local level focus on methods for encouraging collaboration, information-sharing, and transparency.

Remove Barriers That Restrict Access to the Information Needed to Support Youth in Foster Care

Given the mobility of youth in foster care, educators and caseworkers are often in a situation in which their decisions could benefit from information they lack access to—either data from other organizations within their own system or data from a different system. Both education and child welfare systems emphasize privacy and have rules governing the transfer of information that both systems tend to interpret conservatively. Caseworkers, teachers, counselors, and many other stakeholders providing services to youth in foster care could have a clearer picture of students and their needs with access to information about attendance, grades, IEPs, test scores, and notes from past caseworkers.

Facilitating data-sharing within the bounds of state and federal law would ensure that districts have up-to-date information about students entering their schools. This can aid in avoiding gaps in instruction or supplemental services and might help lessen the pressure on youth in foster care to advocate on their own behalf. In addition, alleviating some of the daily barriers faced by caseworkers and providing more-flexible solutions might also improve the turnover rate. This might include, for example, allowing caseworkers the opportunity to work remotely; improving access to information and communication technology services (such as tablets); and offering resources to equip caseworkers to address difficult topics, such as conversations related to diversity, equity, and inclusion and how these issues affect youth experience in school and foster care.

Incentivize and Facilitate Cross-System Communication and Social Engagement

Our case studies illustrated that social engagement can form a useful basis for future collaboration around consistent policy implementation, as well as case management. Regional and local actors might consider providing opportunities for local and regional representatives from both systems to have recurrent opportunities to network. Although this is a seemingly intuitive recommendation, our case study analyses indicated that such social engagement provides an essential foundation for future collaboration to support youth. Furthermore, ensuring that liaison roles at the regional, district, and school levels are filled and that contact information is readily available can help facilitate communication where needed. Nonprofits and community-based organizations also hold the potential to fulfill bridging roles, facilitating communication between systems to support case management.

Designate a Contact or Hotline for Youth or Caregivers Who Need Assistance with School Stability Concerns

Sometimes, youth in foster care or their caregivers are in the best position to advocate for the interests of the student. Therefore, we suggest that regional and local agencies consider creating opportunities for youth and their caregivers to raise concerns about school placement or supports in ways that can elevate their concerns and facilitate change, as necessary. Given high rates of turnover among caseworkers, this type of communication outlet might allow youth and their caregivers to quickly address any challenges or complaints and mitigate educational disruptions for youth in foster care.

State Level

The local actors described above are stretched thin, and many school districts may serve few students in foster care at any point in time. Templates, examples, and standard operating procedures can make it easier for local actors to collaborate effectively and relieve them of the burden of creating such procedures from scratch. Our analysis of state-level data indicates that there may be gaps in the codification of dispute resolution, joint guidance, and the formalization of tools and procedures. In addition, the training of caseworkers in education remains a primary challenge in our case studies. We suggest that states consider the following approaches. In pursuing these options, states do not need to start from scratch but can build on the efforts of states that have already taken action in some of these areas.

Require Written Dispute Resolution for Service Provisions Related to Youth in Foster Care

While the McKinney-Vento Act provides examples of dispute resolution for students experiencing homelessness, ESSA is less directive when it comes to students in foster care. Although Title I, Part A, does not require states to develop dispute resolution procedures, non-regulatory guidance from both the Department of Education and the Department of Health and Human Services strongly encourages the development of such procedures to govern disputes related to children in foster care.[1] We suggest that states establish clear written guidelines for dispute resolution to assist school districts and the child welfare agency in overcoming obstacles facing youth in foster care. Codifying these procedures will allow districts to more effectively assist these students in decisions such as placement. Notable examples include Washington's Dispute Resolutions (Mueller, 2021) and the National Association for the Education of Homeless Children and Youth, Title I, Part A, Foster Care Sample Dispute Resolutions (National Association for the Education of Homeless Children and Youth, 2016).

Provide Joint Guidance Defining and Serving Youth in Foster Care

States should consider providing joint guidance surrounding common issues encountered by education and child welfare stakeholders, such as definitions of what foster care terminology does and does not include, processes surrounding best interest determination, best practices for transportation issues, and guidance on potential funding mechanisms, as well as POCs at the district, county, and regional levels. State guidance should focus on filling common gaps in interpretation and ensure that the same questions or issues do not need to be repeatedly addressed.

Provide Statewide, Standard Tools, Procedures, and Definitions

ESSA encourages collaboration among SEAs, school districts, and child welfare agencies to support youth in foster care but does not specify how this collaboration should occur. As a result, states have a great deal of autonomy to designate their procedures and tools on how they support youth in foster care. In some cases, this autonomy trickles down to the local level; each county child welfare agency or school district has unique processes and tools that may not speak to neighboring agencies or districts. For instance, to facilitate best interest determinations, some districts may use a checklist or review the student's education passport to decide on the optimal placement for the student. Variation across counties or districts, however, might

---

[1] Non-regulatory guidance encourages SEAs, LEAs, and child welfare to collaborate and create dispute-resolution procedures (U.S. Department of Education and U.S. Department of Health and Human Services, 2016, p. 15).

contribute to challenges faced by students as they change placements and school assignments. Therefore, procedures to facilitate communication and information-sharing as part of placement changes might be more effective if those procedures are standardized and formalized across the state.

Data-sharing is an area in which the state could play a particularly important role in promoting standard procedures and definitions that would enable meaningful action at the local level. Although many states have laws, MOUs, or interagency agreements that provide for and facilitate the transfer of data, there is still room for improvement given the conservative approach to information-sharing on the part of local entities within each system. Even when data-sharing agreements are in place, definitions and metrics might vary across the systems, increasing the risk of misunderstandings and limiting the utility of the data. We encourage states to spearhead efforts to develop common definitions and metrics that facilitate information-sharing and use.

Include Educational Outcomes for Youth in Foster Care as School Accountability Indicators

As the aphorism goes, "what gets measured gets done." Our case analysis highlights the importance of data- and information-sharing, as well as the prioritization of the goal of improving the educational opportunities and outcomes of youth in foster care. ESSA requires data on student achievement regarding assessments and graduation rates but allows states to designate another performance indicator of their choosing. Therefore, states can choose indicators that are important to them, and districts will need to create mechanisms to report on these specific indicators. We suggest that states consider identifying youth in foster care as a specified subgroup in examining educational outcomes and opportunity gaps. In particular, holding schools accountable for the performance of this (often transient) population of students might help encourage schools and districts to focus on supporting youth in foster care. These indicators could also be beneficial to child welfare agencies, such as their required annual Adoption and Foster Care Analysis and Reporting System report, which now includes data on school enrollment, highest grade completed, and participation in special education (U.S. Department of Health and Human Services, 2020).

Include Youth-Centered Data Metrics

Although the best interest determination should typically include the youth in foster care, their caseworker, biological parent, guardian, or foster parents, the implementation and accountability of these processes differ by school district. Currently, only 12 states and the District of Columbia require the youth to be included in the process (Child Welfare Information Gateway, 2020, p. 4). We encourage states to create data metrics to (1) ensure that the youth is an active participant in the placement decision and (2) assist the youth in ensuring that they are meeting all the necessary milestones and overcoming daily barriers, such as absenteeism and coursework completion rates.

Furthermore, ensuring that a youth in foster care is asked their opinion on the placement decision, with consideration to the "age and level of maturity of the child to express a reasonable preference," may also serve as a proxy of cross-system collaboration, as the youth provides the one touchpoint that both systems aspire to serve (Child Welfare Information Gateway, 2020, p. 4). This will also provide the youth with a setting in which to discuss why they would prefer to stay or move and allow them to be a part of the decisionmaking process.

To formalize this effort, we encourage use of an actionable indicator to track progress, such as making participation of the youth a requirement for the best-interest-determination meeting, if the youth is willing. Although the disaggregated graduation and student achievement metrics have been instrumental ESSA provisions, these requirements provide a big-picture overview regarding completion rates and assessment trends among youth in foster care but do not provide data on areas with which the youth may currently need help. Therefore, as is done in California, we encourage metrics that can readily assist youth in foster care and those who assist them during their schooling. For instance, some of California's outcome data requirements include "attendance, absenteeism, suspension, expulsion, rates of A-G coursework completion, and advanced placement completion rates" (Alliance for Child's Rights, 2016, p. 34).[2] In practice, these additional data aid in ensuring that students do not fall through the cracks. High absen-

---

[2] *A-G coursework* refers to a series of classes required for high school graduation.

teeism, suspension, and expulsion rates are indicators of dropout risk and might be mitigated. Additionally, coursework completion rates might aid in ensuring that students are on track for graduation.

Integrate Basic Education Stability Training into Caseworker Preparation

Limited preparatory training for caseworkers in supporting school stability and educational opportunities presented a major challenge across our case studies. In many states, educational stability is not a part of the professional learning requirements specified in state licensure requirements for caseworkers. We encourage states to consider including educational stability and support as part of training, licensing, or continuing education requirements to ensure that caseworkers have exposure to the nuances of the field, such as the best-interest-determination processes and the rights and protections that students in foster care must have under ESSA.

Federal Level

Federal policy provides a framework that guides and influences state and local efforts. Our analysis of federal policy around supporting the educational opportunities and outcomes of youth in foster care illuminated the similarities and differences between ESSA and the McKinney-Vento Act. We suggest that the existing foundation of federal legislation could be strengthened toward this goal through designation of additional funding mechanisms specifically to serve this population of students. Furthermore, our analysis of the variation among state legislation and governance, as well as the commonalities in experience with collaboration and promising practices, suggests that mechanisms to facilitate and promote sharing of best practice among states would be a worthy investment.

Allocate a Designated Funding Mechanism for Students in Foster Care

At present, funding to support students in foster care remains unspecified. Although Title I is a potential source for districts and states to use, it is difficult to imagine LEAs prioritizing the use of this funding source, which is intended to support disadvantaged students generally, for the very small population of students in foster care without a specific, mandated allocation for this group. Increasing Title I funding overall could be a potential solution, but past efforts to substantially increase this funding have met resistance. Increasing the level of Title I funding overall would not guarantee that the additional resources would be used to support students in foster care. Alternatively, one approach may be to mandate, at a federal level, a separate program that provides specific funding for service provisions related to assisting youth in foster care, similar to McKinney-Vento's provisions for people experiencing homelessness.

Use and Encourage Best Practices That Have Worked for Other States

This analysis has highlighted several promising practices states use to promote collaboration and support education for youth in foster care. It is evident that states face common challenges, despite their differences, and are innovating in this important area. We suggest that structures to promote the sharing of promising practices across states may be beneficial. At present, the non-regulatory joint guidance highlights best practices through real-world examples but does not identify which state implemented these successful strategies (U.S. Department of Education and U.S. Department of Health and Human Services, 2016). Enhanced transparency may allow for more-authentic and more-meaningful sharing. Additionally, many states have successfully implemented legislation to mitigate common barriers and ensure that others in the future do not face the same obstacles. Although the feasibility of specific legislation may vary across states, these examples present opportunities for other states to replicate or innovate policy solutions. To that end, a centralized repository and opportunities for cross-state sharing hold promise to catalyze further improvement.

Directions for Future Research

This study was motivated by the limited scholarship on this important topic. Our initial analysis has illuminated several areas in which additional research would contribute to discourse and improvement efforts in the field. A detailed, systemic policy review of the varied definitions across states and across agencies within a state, foster care, and key aspects of transitions might help to show where challenges arise in collaboration because of policy incoherence.

We also suggest deeper inquiry into the benefits and drawbacks of consistent school placement to understand the factors that influence best placement for young people, as well as an exploration of how caseworkers engage in supporting the educational opportunities and outcomes of young people.

Additionally, we suggest that, although within-state transitions are most common, it might be worth examining how school transitions and data-sharing occur when a young person is placed across state lines.

Additional Detail on Data and Methods

This study began with a literature and data scan and engagement with an external advisory panel. The panel consisted of seven individuals in six organizations who play different roles supporting the educational outcomes of youth in foster care and bring different perspectives to the topic. These individuals worked for federal, state, and local organizations in the education and child welfare sectors. These were government, advocacy, and philanthropic organizations. We convened the advisory panel in December 2021 to solicit feedback on our initial data collection, case study research design, and selection. We reconvened the panel in September 2022 to solicit feedback on our preliminary findings. Feedback from the external advisory panel informed the theoretical framework, guiding questions, and case selection methods. In addition, the panel reviewed and provided comments on this publication.

RAND researchers gathered data on governance, funding, enrollment, safety and permanence, and key policies for both the education and child welfare systems in all U.S. states, the District of Columbia, and territories. These data were analyzed to examine the prevalence and variation of governance arrangements across the country and informed case study selection. We also conducted a systematic review of federal legislation governing the education of youth in foster care. Our policy review and data scan relied on several sources of information across the states.

Governance

We categorized each state's education governance structure as state, county, or local based on a two-part test. First, we used data compiled by the Education Commission of the States about power and duties of the chief state school officer (Education Commission of the States, 2020a), the state board of education (Education Commission of the States, 2020c), and school boards (Education Commission of the States, 2020b). These data were based on the 2017 Census of Governments, state description data (U.S. Census Bureau, 2019), to characterize the states by where operational responsibility for education system operation rests. State constitutions and legislation assign specific duties to different roles within the system. Second, as needed, we turned to supplementary data sources—namely, state statutes—to make a final determination. Ten states had only one designation (state, county, or local) across the sources, while the rest had multiple designations reflecting a hybrid of either regional and local governance or county and local governance. For states with multiple designations, we used the ratio of districts to counties to categorize the governance as primarily local, state, or county: below 1 = state, 1 to 5 = county, and more than 5 = local.

There was limited literature on the governance of child welfare systems. To categorize the governance arrangement of this system, we relied on information from the Child Welfare Information Gateway, an effort of the Children's Bureau, an office within the U.S. Department of Health and Human Services (Child Welfare Information Gateway, undated). The governance categorization captures "the degree of centralization of authority, and responsibility for child welfare funding, policymaking, licensing, training for workers and more." It is based on 2017 Children's Bureau data, as well as information from states' Child and Family Services Plans regarding the objectives, vision, and goals for their child welfare programs (Child Welfare Information Gateway, 2018).

Funding and Expenditure

We compiled information about FY 2018 federal, state, and local funding and expenditures for the child welfare and education systems by state. Child welfare system data captured major funding sources, such as Title IV, Part E, and Title IV, Part B, of the Social Security Act (Pub. L. 74-271, 1935), Medicaid, Social Service Block Grant, Temporary Assistance for Needy Families, and other federal sources (Rosinsky et al., 2021; Children's Bureau, 2021).[1] For the education system, we accessed data, federal, local, and total revenue and expenditures for each state (National Center for Education Statistics, 2022b; Hanson, 2022).[2]

Enrollment

Enrollment measures provide a sense of the size of each system and the relative size of the child welfare and education systems in each state. We obtained education system enrollment data by state, region, and LEA from the National Center for Education Statistics for the 2020–2021 school year (National Center for Education Statistics, 2017; National Center for Education Statistics, 2020). For child welfare, we used state enrollment data about the numbers of children in foster care (FY 2020) and entering foster care (FY 2020), as well as the maltreatment victim rate for 2019 (Children's Bureau, 2021).

Safety and Permanency

To understand how basic outcomes vary for children interacting with the child welfare system across states, we pulled data from a number of data sources to create indicators for maltreatment (Children's Bureau, undated-

---

[1] Regarding how expenditures are defined within the Child Trends report, "the Child Welfare Financing Survey specifically asked states for their expenditures in [school FY] 2018, as opposed to amounts that may have been appropriated but not actually expended" (Rosinsky et al., 2021).

[2] The National Center for Education Statistics defines *federal revenue* as "the subtotal of all Federal Sources of Revenue categories." *Total revenue* is defined as the sum "of subtotals for Local Government, State Government, Intermediate Government Agencies, and Federal Government. Does not include other sources of revenue." And *local revenue* is "the sum of Local Revenues and Revenues from Intermediate Agencies." *Total expenditure* is defined as the sum of "Total Expenditure: for Education, Direct State Support Expenditures for Private School Students, and Interest on long term debt" (National Center for Education Statistics, 2022b).

a), time to adoption (Children's Bureau, undated-b), and the number of placements (Children's Bureau, undated-c).

Indicators of Collaboration

We also used existing documentation of collaborative activities or features across the states. For this analysis, sources consisted of the following:

- state guidelines and funding priorities and categorizations of states based on whether their school accountability systems require reporting on the subgroup of youth in foster care—if foster care status is a student population subgroup designed for accountability reporting and state education funding formulas (Education Commission of the States, 2020a; Education Commission of the States, 2020b; Education Commission of the States, 2020c)
- information from the Data Quality Campaign about whether education system and child welfare system data on youth in foster care can be linked (Data Quality Campaign, 2016)
- information from the National Conference of State Legislatures to identify states that had state-specific legislation emphasizing educational continuity or stability for youth in foster care, data-sharing between systems or child welfare, and education collaboration prior to Fostering Connection (National Conference of State Legislatures, 2016)
- state education policy tracking through the Education Commission of the States (Education Commission of the States, 2021b)
- the Legal Center for Foster Care and Education, which serves as a central hub for agencies seeking assistance and tools to serve their youth in foster care and improve their educational outcomes; one of their many resources is a repository of state tools, inclusive of interagency agreements and MOUs (we reviewed whether states had a current or prior interagency agreement or MOU within their database) (Legal Center for Foster Care and Education, undated)
- recommendations from advisory board members on promising collaboration practices in states that might warrant additional follow-up.

State, County, and District Case Studies

Four case study states were selected to reflect variation in governance arrangements, size, and geographic region. Within each of these four states, we selected two counties that represented diversity in urbanicity and four districts (two in each county, where appropriate) that similarly demonstrated variation in urbanicity and size. We reached out for interviews with a state, county or regional, and district or local representative from both education and child welfare agencies in these states. In total, we reached out to 39 individuals to request participation in interviews; 13 individuals agreed to participate.

Sampling Criteria

Initially, we selected six states for qualitative data collection: Washington, Georgia, California, Wisconsin, Hawaii, and North Carolina. These cases were purposefully sampled to represent variation in levels of collaboration based on existing indicators, the degree of decentralization and alignment (see Table A.1), the degree of fragmentation of the education system as reflected in the district-to-county ratio, and geographic variation.

Within the states selected for further study, we also explored within-state variation by looking at the ratio of the number of schools to number of school districts or LEAs. At the district level, we reviewed population size, type of locale (rural, town, city, or suburbs), and demographics (race and ethnicity of the student body and median household income). At the county level, we looked at the U.S. Department of Agriculture Rural-Urban Continuum Code, population size, and the ratio of children in foster care placement to the county population (National Center for Education Statistics, undated-a; U.S. Department of Agriculture, 2020; National Center for Education Statistics, 2021).

At the county level, the ratio of children in foster care (using the last available dataset for the past fiscal year) to county population was used, and we prioritized the largest ratios of children to foster care in both metro and nonmetro areas and the variability in the Rural-Urban Continuum Code, and population size within potential counties. The ratios ranged from 0.0099, a nonmetro rural county with a population under 5,000 individu-

TABLE A.1
Case Study Sampling Criteria

State	Level of Governance (Education and Child Welfare)	Ratio of District to County	Summary
Washington	Local and state	9	• Level of governance: local (education) and state (child welfare) • Ratio of district to counties: 9; allowing for a midsized ratio to compare across other states • Notable collaboration indicators: (a) an MOU on record between the Department of Social and Health Services and the Washington State Office of Superintendent of Public Instruction and (b) past legislation referencing educational stability or continuity and information-sharing • Additional notes: the only state recommended by two individuals within our technical advisory group
California	Local and county administered	37	• Level of governance: local (education) and county (child welfare) • Ratio of district to counties: 37; serving as our largest ratio to compare across other states • Notable collaboration indicators: (a) an interagency agreement within Solano County, (b) a state dashboard, (c) past legislation referencing educational stability or continuity and information-sharing, and (d) foster care status within accountability systems and supplemental funding • Additional notes: a number of our technical advisory members are located in California, which might lend to them assisting us with notable sites and individuals we may contact

Table A.1—Continued

State	Level of Governance (Education and Child Welfare)	Ratio of District to County	Summary
Georgia	County and state	2	• Level of governance: county (education) and state (child welfare) • Ratio of district to counties: 2; serving as one of our smaller ratios to compare across other states • Notable collaboration indicators: past legislation referencing educational stability or continuity and information-sharing
Hawaii	State and state	0	• Level of governance: state (education) and state (child welfare) • Ratio of district to counties: 0; only state that has this categorization of governance and ratio of district to counties • Notable collaboration indicators: not applicable • Additional notes: Hawaii was removed from consideration as a potential case study site due to unsuccessful outreach attempts
North Carolina	County and county	2	• Level of governance: county (education) and county (child welfare) • Ratio of district to counties: 2; serving as one of our smaller ratios to compare across other states • Notable collaboration indicators: not applicable • Additional notes: North Carolina was removed from consideration as a potential case study site due to unsuccessful outreach attempts
Wisconsin	Local and hybrid	6	• Level of governance: local (education) and hybrid (child welfare) • Ratio of district to counties: 6; serving as one of our midsized ratios to compare across other states • Notable collaboration indicators: according to Data Quality Campaign (2014), there is evidence of linkage between education and foster care data systems

als, to the smallest ratio, 0.0020, a metro county with about 1 million individuals. The average ratio of children in foster care to population given our four states' corresponding counties was 0.0036. We selected four counties within each of the six states, purposefully sampled to represent variation in (1) metro and nonmetro categories within the National Center for Health Statistics Urban–Rural Classification Scheme for Counties (Centers for Disease Control and Prevention, 2017), (2) population size, (3) degree of centralization of the child welfare system as reflected by the ratio of children in foster care to the population, (4) geographic variation, and (5) variation in terms of the degree of decentralization and alignment regarding the chosen states.

We prioritized the inclusion of metro and nonmetro counties for each state and the highest proportionality of children in foster care to the population within each district. Due to the lack of variability in the Rural-Urban Continuum Code, states with the smallest number of counties were chosen first.

At the district level, we explored the demographic information of the student body and the median household income of families residing within that district. Given our options, we prioritized selecting the most-diverse metro and nonmetro districts as they pertain to race and ethnicity and prioritized variability concerning median household incomes. We examined data on school districts by county and selected up to two districts in each. In some counties, there was only one district. We excluded Department of Defense Education Activity and private schools from consideration. To the extent that we had choices, we considered (1) student enrollment, selecting the district with the largest enrollment and one other district, and (2) locale and demographics, selecting one metro and one nonmetro county in each state. Within each category, after identifying the district with the largest enrollment, we selected a second district to obtain variation in demographic characteristics and locale type while still being large enough to plausibly have youth in foster care enrolled.

Participant Recruitment

We reached out to a number of education and child welfare stakeholders within our case study states. Respondents and contact information were gleaned from publicly available agency websites (e.g., state departments of education; departments of children, youth, and families). After initial recruitment efforts, we noted no responses from Hawaii or North Carolina and removed these two states from our sample and ended any further recruitment efforts.

For the remaining four states, our outreach efforts are summarized in Table A.2. However, despite multiple contact attempts, including emails and phone calls, we had difficulty reaching and engaging stakeholders. Some barriers to reaching stakeholders included, but were not limited to, incorrect publicly listed contact information, inaccurate POCs (outdated listings or listed as vacancies), and concerns about needing agency permission to participate in research.

We successfully conducted interviews with stakeholders in education and child welfare agencies at the state, district, and county or regional levels. A summary of the completed interviews by category and system can be seen in Table A.3. By category, 53 percent of all of our interviewees held state-level positions. By system, 67 percent of our stakeholders were education

TABLE A.2

Case Study Outreach Efforts to Individuals

	By Category			By State			
	State	District	County or Region	Calif.	Ga.	Wash.	Wisc.
Attempted contacts	11	14	15	10	9	11	10
No responses	3	10	7	3	5	5	6
Declined contacts	0	2	4	2	2	1	2
Interviews completed	8	2	4	5	2	5	2
Response rate	73%	14%	27%	50%	22%	45%	20%

TABLE A.3

Completed Interviews

	By Category			By System	
	State	District	County or Region	Education	Child Welfare
California	3	0	2	5	0
Georgia	1	0	1	1	1
Washington	2	1	2	2	3
Wisconsin	1	1	0	2	0
Total	7	2	5	10	4

system representatives. All participants served the needs of youth in foster care as at least part of their roles and responsibilities in their agencies.

In addition, we reached out to advocacy organizations for youth in foster care and university support programs for adults who have been in foster care in all four case states. Through these organizations, we invited adults (older than 18 years of age) who had previously experienced foster care to join focus groups about their experience with the education and child welfare systems. In total, we conducted group interviews with 12 individuals.

RAND researchers conducted these semistructured interviews and focus groups from May 2022 through September 2022, via a video conference platform. All interviews were audio-recorded and transcribed. Transcribed data were then coded using a combination of deductively and inductively determined codes. These codes included descriptive codes about the cases (e.g., state, governance arrangement), thematic codes about the key topics of collaboration (e.g., placement decisions, transportation, case management), and analytic codes derived from the literature on collaboration (e.g., shared goals, communication structures, formalization). We used cross-case meta-matrices to engage in systematic data reduction and to look for patterns across our case study sites. We then conducted analytic memoing, focusing on both within-case and across-case themes. Where possible, we triangulated interview findings with documentation.

We consider this study exploratory in nature. There are limitations to the generalizability and validity of our data. First, we sampled just four states as case studies, given capacity constraints. Given the variation in policy and contexts across the country, our findings may not represent the experience of all states, counties, or local agencies. Second, we were unable to recruit participants across all levels of each case study system and did not sample representatives from nonprofits or community-based organizations who may commonly work with both systems. We believe that competing demands on time, particularly in the COVID-19 pandemic period, might have prohibited potential participants from joining the study. Therefore, we cannot systematically draw conclusions about cross- and within-system collaboration in all of the case study states. Finally, our qualitative data collection draws on perception data, which may or may not fully reflect actual practice.

Abbreviations

AB	assembly bill
COVID-19	coronavirus disease 2019
ESEA	Elementary and Secondary Education Act
ESSA	Every Student Succeeds Act
FY	fiscal year
IEP	Individualized Education Plan
K–12	kindergarten through grade 12
LEA	local education agency
MOU	memorandum of understanding
POC	point of contact
SEA	state education agency

References

Alliance for Children's Rights, *Foster Youth Education Toolkit*, December 2016.

Ayscue, Jennifer B., and Gary Orfield, "School District Lines Stratify Educational Opportunity by Race and Poverty," *Race and Social Problems*, Vol. 7, No. 1, May 2015.

Bardach, Eugene, "Turf Barriers to Interagency Collaboration," in Donald F. Kettl and H. Brinton Milward, eds., *The State of Public Management*, Johns Hopkins University Press, 1996.

Barrat, Vanessa X., and BethAnn Berliner, *The Invisible Achievement Gap: Education Outcomes of Students in Foster Care in California's Public Schools*, WestEd, 2013.

Bronstein, Laura R., "A Model for Interdisciplinary Collaboration," *Social Work*, Vol. 48, No. 3, July 2003.

Burns, Dion, Danny Espinoza, Julie Adams, and Naomi Ondrasek, *California Students in Foster Care: Challenges and Promising Practices*, Learning Policy Institute, July 26, 2022.

California State Assembly, Educational Rights and Stability for Foster Youth Act, Assembly Bill 490, October 12, 2003

California State Assembly, Public Social Services: Foster Care: Funding, Assembly Bill 403, February 19, 2015.

California State Assembly, Foster Youth: Trauma-Informed System of Care, Assembly Bill 2083, February 7, 2018.

Capacity Building Center for States, *Creating and Sustaining Cross-System Collaboration to Support Families in Child Welfare with Co-Occurring Issues: An Administrator's Handbook*, Children's Bureau, Administration for Children and Families, U.S. Department of Health and Human Services, 2017.

Centers for Disease Control and Prevention, "NCHS Urban-Rural Classification Scheme for Counties," webpage, last updated June 1, 2017. As of February 20, 2023:
https://www.cdc.gov/nchs/data_access/urban_rural.htm

Chen, Grace, "Parental Involvement Is Key to Student Success," *Public School Review*, last updated May 20, 2022.

Child Trends, "Child Welfare Financing SFY 2018: State-Level Data Table," spreadsheet, March 9, 2021.

Child Welfare Information Gateway, "About Child Welfare Information Gateway," webpage, U.S. Department of Health and Human Services, undated. As of January 18, 2023:
https://www.childwelfare.gov/aboutus/

Child Welfare Information Gateway, *State vs. County Administration of Child Welfare Services*, U.S. Department of Health and Human Services, March 2018.

Child Welfare Information Gateway, *Determining the Best Interests of the Child*, U.S. Department of Health and Human Services, June 2020.

Child Welfare Information Gateway, "Numbers of Children Adopted, by State," spreadsheet, U.S. Department of Health and Human Services, last updated October 4, 2021.

Children's Bureau, "Outcomes 1 and 2: Safety," webpage, U.S. Department of Health and Human Services, undated-a. As of September 22, 2022:
https://cwoutcomes.acf.hhs.gov/cwodatasite/recurrence/index

Children's Bureau, "Outcome 5: Time to Adoption," webpage, U.S. Department of Health and Human Services, undated-b. As of September 22, 2022:
https://cwoutcomes.acf.hhs.gov/cwodatasite/fiveOne/index

Children's Bureau, "Outcome 6: Placement and Stability," webpage, U.S. Department of Health and Human Services, undated-c. As of September 22, 2022:
https://cwoutcomes.acf.hhs.gov/cwodatasite/sixOneLessThan12/index

Children's Bureau, "AFCARS State Data Tables 2010 Through 2020," spreadsheet, U.S. Department of Health and Human Services, October 4, 2021.

Children's Bureau, *The AFCARS Report*, U.S. Department of Health and Human Services, Report No. 29, November 1, 2022.

Clemens, Elysia V., Trent L. Lalonde, and Alison Phillips Sheesley, "The Relationship Between School Mobility and Students in Foster Care Earning a High School Credential," *Children and Youth Services Review*, Vol. 68, September 2016.

Code of Federal Regulations, Title 34, Education; Subtitle B, Regulations of the Offices of the Department of Education; Chapter III, Office of Special Education and Rehabilitative Services, Department of Education; Part 303, Early Intervention Program for Infants and Toddlers with Disabilities; Subpart A, General; Subpart 23; Local Education Agency.

Data Quality Campaign, "Supporting Students in Foster Care," fact sheet, March 24, 2016.

Education Commission of the States, "K–12 Governance: Chief State School Officer," spreadsheet, November 2020a.

Education Commission of the States, "K–12 Governance: School Boards," spreadsheet, November 2020b.

Education Commission of the States, "K–12 Governance: State Board of Education," spreadsheet, November 2020c.

Education Commission of the States, "K–12 and Special Education Funding 2021," spreadsheet, October 2021a.

Education Commission of the States, "States' School Accountability Systems 2021," spreadsheet, December 2021b.

Garstka, Teri A., Alice Lieberman, Jacklyn Biggs, Betsy Thompson, and Michelle Marie Levy, "Barriers to Cross-Systems Collaboration in Child Welfare, Education, and the Courts: Supporting Educational Well-Being of Youth in Care Through Systems Change," *Journal of Public Child Welfare*, Vol. 8, No. 2, May 8, 2014.

Goodman, Christopher B., "Local Government Fragmentation: What Do We Know?" *State and Local Government Review*, Vol. 51, No. 2, June 2019.

Hage, Jerald, and Michael Aiken, "Relationship of Centralization to Other Structural Properties," *Administrative Science Quarterly*, Vol. 12, No. 1, June 1967.

Hanson, Melanie, "U.S. Public Education Spending Statistics," webpage, Education Data Initiative, June 15, 2022. As of January 18, 2023: https://educationdata.org/public-education-spending-statistics

Henderson, Anne T., and Karen L. Mapp, eds., *A New Wave of Evidence: The Impact of School, Family, and Community Connections on Student Achievement, Annual Synthesis*, Southwest Educational Development Laboratory, 2002.

Herbert, James, Nicholas Ghan, Mary Salveron, and Wendy Walsh, "Possible Factors Supporting Cross-Agency Collaboration in Child Abuse Cases: A Scoping Review," *Journal of Child Sexual Abuse*, Vol. 30, No. 2, 2021.

Hlavac, George C., and Edward J. Easterly, "FERPA Primer: The Basics and Beyond," *NACE Journal*, April 1, 2015.

Hyland, Shelley S., and Elizabeth Davis, *Local Police Departments, 2016: Personnel*, U.S. Department of Justice, NCJ 252835, October 2019.

Klein, Alyson, and Andrew Ujifusa, "New ESSA Spending Regulations Proposed," *EducationWeek*, September 16, 2016.

Krimmel, John T., "The Northern York County Police Consolidation Experience: An Analysis of the Consolidation of Police Services in Eight Pennsylvania Rural Communities," *Policing: An International Journal of Police Strategies and Management*, Vol. 20, No. 3, 1997.

Langworthy, Sara, and Anita Larson, *Collaboration Across Minnesota Child Welfare and Education Systems*, University of Minnesota Extension, Center for Family Development, 2014.

Langworthy, Sara, and Lauren Robertson, *Get the Data, Share the Data, Use the Data Recommendations from the Three-State Child Welfare and Education Learning Community (CWELC) Project*, University of Minnesota Extension, Center for Family Development, 2014.

Legal Center for Foster Care and Education, database, undated. As of September 22, 2022:
https://fostercareandeducation.org/Database.aspx

Legal Center for Foster Care and Education, *Highlights of Joint Federal Guidance to Ensure School Success for Students in Foster Care Under the ESSA*, 2016.

Legal Center for Foster Care and Education and National Center for Homeless Education, "Best Practices: School Selection for Students in Out-of-Home Care," 2009.

Martin, Lawrence L., and Jeannie Hock Schiff, "City-County Consolidations: Promise Versus Performance," *State and Local Government Review*, Vol. 43, No. 2, August 2011.

McKellar, Nancy, and Katherine C. Cowen, "Supporting Students in Foster Care," *Principal Leadership*, September 2011.

McNaught, Kathleen, and Emily Peeler, "Every Student Succeeds Means Children in Foster Care Too: State Progress on ESSA's Foster Care Provisions," *Child Law Practice*, Vol. 36, No. 6, November 2017.

Mueller, Martin, *Foster Care Education Program: Dispute Resolution Process*, Washington Office of Superintendent of Public Instruction, 2021.

National Association for the Education of Homeless Children and Youth, *Title I, Part A Foster Care Sample Dispute Resolution Process*, September 2016.

National Center for Education Statistics, "ACS-ED: District Demographic Dashboard 2016–20," dataset dashboard, U.S. Department of Education, undated-a. As of February 17, 2023:
https://nces.ed.gov/programs/edge/acsdashboard

National Center for Education Statistics, "Search for Public School Districts," database, U.S. Department of Education, undated-b. As of January 19, 2023:
https://nces.ed.gov/ccd/districtsearch/index.asp

National Center for Education Statistics, "Table 5.10. Percent and Number of Children Enrolled in State Prekindergarten Programs, by State: 2016–17," webpage, U.S. Department of Education, 2017. As of February 28, 2023: https://nces.ed.gov/programs/statereform/tab5_10.asp

National Center for Education Statistics, "Enrollment in Public Elementary and Secondary Schools, by Region, State, and Jurisdiction: Selected Years, Fall 1990 Through Fall 2029," U.S. Department of Education, 2020. As of September 22, 2022: https://nces.ed.gov/programs/digest/d20/tables/dt20_203.20.asp

National Center for Education Statistics, "Back-to-School Statistics," webpage, U.S. Department of Education, 2022a. As of January 19, 2023: https://nces.ed.gov/fastfacts/display.asp?id=372

National Center for Education Statistics, *Public School Expenditures. Condition of Education*, U.S. Department of Education, May 2022b.

National Center for Homeless Education, *Federal Data Summary School Years 2014–15 to 2016–17*, February 2019.

National Conference of State Legislatures, *Educating Children in Foster Care State Legislation 2008–2015*, September 27, 2016.

Pecora, Peter J., "Maximizing Educational Achievement of Youth in Foster Care and Alumni: Factors Associated with Success," *Children and Youth Services Review*, Vol. 34, No. 6, June 2012.

Pecora, Peter J., Ronald C. Kessler, Jason Williams, Kirk O'Brien, A. Chris Downs, Diana English, James White, Eva Hiripi, Catherine Roller White, Tamera Wiggins, and Kate Holmes, *Improving Family Foster Care: Findings from the Northwest Foster Care Alumni Study*, Casey Family Programs, 2005.

Pecora, Peter J., and Kirk O'Brien, "Fostering Success in Education: Educational Outcomes of Students in Foster Care," in Patricia McNamara, Carme Montserrat, and Sarah Wise, eds., *Education in Out-of-Home Care: International Perspectives on Policy, Practice and Research*, Springer International Publishing, 2019.

Public Law 74-271, Social Security Act, August 14, 1935.

Public Law 89-10, Elementary and Secondary Education Act, April 11, 1965.

Public Law 100-77, McKinney-Vento Homeless Assistance Act, July 22, 1987.

Public Law 110-351, Fostering Connections to Success and Increasing Adoptions Act, October 7, 2008.

Public Law 114-95, Every Student Succeeds Act, December 10, 2015.

Revised Code of Washington, Title 28a, Chapter 320, Section 148, Foster Care Liaison—Building Point of Contact, 2018.

Rosinsky, Kristina, Sarah Catherine Williams, Megan Fischer, and Maggie Haas, *Child Welfare Financing SFY 2018: A Survey of Federal, State, and Local Expenditures*, Child Trends, March 2021.

Schomburg, Aysha E., and Ruth Ryder, "Academic Success for Students in Foster Care Begins with Strong Partnership Between Child Welfare and Education Systems," *Homeroom: The Official Blog of the U.S. Department of Education*, July 6, 2022.

Sciamanna, John, "Less Than 2 in 5 Children Now Covered by Federal Foster Care Funding," Child Welfare League of America, undated.

Simon, Herbert A., *The New Science of Management Decision*, Harper & Brothers, 1960.

Snyder, Thomas D., Rachel Dinkes, William Sonnenberg, and Stephen Cornman, *Study of the Title I, Part A Grant Program Mathematical Formulas*, National Center for Education Statistics, 2019.

Social Security Administration, "Definitions, Compilation of Social Security Laws §475," undated.

Stoltzfus, Emilie, *Child Welfare: Purposes, Federal Programs, and Funding*, Congressional Research Service, 2019.

Stone, Susan, Amy D'andrade, and Michael Austin, "Educational Services for Children in Foster Care: Common and Contrasting Perspectives of Child Welfare and Education Stakeholders," *Journal of Public Child Welfare*, Vol. 1, No. 2, 2007.

Stringer, Kate, "The State of America's Foster Care Students: How the Every Student Succeeds Act Is Designed to Better Understand and Support These 430,000 Kids," The 74, July 25, 2018.

Trinidad, Justin, and Hailly T. N. Korman, *Truly Universal: Overcoming Barriers to School Choice for Youth in Foster Care*, Bellwether Education, July 2020.

U.S. Census Bureau, *Individual State Descriptions: 2017 Census of Governments*, U.S. Government Printing Office, 2019.

U.S. Department of Agriculture, "2013 Rural-Urban Continuum Codes," spreadsheet, last updated December 10, 2020. As of May 4, 2022: https://www.ers.usda.gov/webdocs/DataFiles/53251/ ruralurbancodes2013.xls?v=4371.2

U.S. Department of Education, *Education for Homeless Children and Youths Program Non-Regulatory Guidance*, 2017.

U.S. Department of Education and U.S. Department of Health and Human Services, *Non-Regulatory Guidance: Ensuring Educational Stability for Children in Foster Care*, 2016.

U.S. Department of Health and Human Services, "Adoption and Foster Care Analysis and Reporting System," *Federal Register*, Vol. 85, No. 92, May 12, 2020.

Washington Office of Superintendent of Public Instruction, *Best Practices: School Selection for Children and Youth in Foster Care*, undated.

Washington State Legislature, Making Supplemental Operating Appropriations, Engrossed Substitute Senate Bill 6032, 2018.

Zetlin, Andrea, Lois Weinberg, and Nancy M. Shea, "Caregivers, School Liaisons, and Agency Advocates Speak Out About the Educational Needs of Children and Youths in Foster Care," *Social Work*, Vol. 55, No 3, July 2010.

Zinth, Kyle, *Parental Involvement in Education*, Education Commission of the States, May 2005.